Careers Services

History, policy and practice in the United Kingdom

David Peck

RoutledgeFalmer
Taylor & Francis Group

LONDON AND NEW YORK

First published 2004 by RoutledgeFalmer
11 New Fetter Lane, London EC4P 4EE

Simultaneously published in the USA and Canada
by RoutledgeFalmer
29 West 35th Street, New York, NY 10001

RoutledgeFalmer is an imprint of the Taylor & Francis Group

© 2004 David Peck

Typeset in Garamond by Keystroke, Jacaranda Lodge, Wolverhampton
Printed and bound in Great Britain by TJ International, Padstow, Cornwall

British Library Cataloguing in Publication Data
A catalogue record for this book is available from the British Library

Library of Congress Cataloging in Publication Data
Peck, David, 1935–
    Careers services : history, policy and practice in the United Kingdom /
David Peck.
        p. cm.
Includes bibliographical references and index.
    1. Vocational guidance–Great Britain–History. I. Title.
    HF5382.5.G7P43 2004
    331.702'0941–dc22   2003025219

ISBN 0–415–33935–9 (hbk)
ISBN 0–415–33936–7 (pbk)

This book is for my grandsons. May they make their decisions wisely and well.

Contents

Foreword

I'd already had three jobs when I entered the Youth Employment Service in 1957 but satisfaction had eluded me. From my beginning in Sheffield's Youth Employment Bureau I was fascinated by the problems people experienced in choosing and finding jobs and absorbed in the task of helping them to choose.

Later, as a vocational guidance officer, I enjoyed the satisfaction of working in and with schools helping individuals and institutions solve their problems. Visiting employers, finding out about jobs and those who succeed in them, finding ways to make this knowledge available to young people, parents and teachers, provided all the stimulus I needed.

Moving to Lincoln to lead its small Youth Employment Service widened my interest further. Contributing to the work of a local education authority and influencing headteachers made me realise the potential of career advice to make a wider contribution. The opportunities provided by the new Careers Service and my move to Shropshire led to my involvement with the national scene through the Institute of Career Guidance and the Heads of Careers Service Association.

I published my first article in 1964 and have written something almost every year since then. The idea of writing this book was first put to me in the early 1980s but began to take shape in about 1997. It would not have come to fruition without the encouragement of a large number of friends and colleagues who have offered advice, ideas and practical help.

First among these I must mention my colleagues at the Centre for Guidance Studies, Tony Watts, Deirdre Hughes and Judith Ayton, who have struggled with my barely legible handwriting and sometimes convoluted prose. They have kept me in touch with the real world. From the wider, real and modern world of career guidance I've had invaluable help from Cynthia Gittins, Lyn Barham, Roger Little, Peter Jones, Geoff Ford, Dermot Dick, Nicky Peck and many others.

Most of all my thanks go to Pat, my wife, who has lived with my enthusiasm through many years and sustained me throughout my unusually long
career.

Acknowledgement

The writing, publication and distribution of this book have been actively supported by the Centre for Guidance Studies at the University of Derby and by the Institute of Career Guidance.

Introduction

Walk down Margaret Street in central Birmingham. Note the stylish art-deco College of Art close to the Victorian Educational Institute where once pupil doctors and dentists attended evening classes, along with pattern-makers and draughtsmen. But, look more closely at the undistinguished building opposite, still the Education office, as it was in the early years of the twentieth century.

The dormer windows in the top storey mark the dormitories which once housed young people in safe, comfortable accommodation while they completed their education and began apprenticeships to skilled trades in the modern industries of an exciting new technological age.

Many were canal children – itinerant, unable to attend schools, whose lives with their parents had been tied to the old extractive industries, but whose horizons had been widened by welfare officers who visited them, interviewed their parents, placed them in suitable training opportunities, arranged their accommodation.

Birmingham wasn't alone in responding to social and economic needs at the turn of the century. In Scotland, Mrs Ogilvie Gordon was planning Educational and Employment Bureaux. Children's Care Committees, Social Side Committees, the National Council of Women, the London Apprenticeship and Skilled Employment Association were working in London and elsewhere to provide wider opportunities and to foster co-operation between schools and employers.

Gerrold Milsted, who retired from his post of Juvenile Employment Officer for Tottenham in 1939, recalled giving career advice and keeping destination records as a teacher in 1899. He believed headteachers and school attendance officers had been active in helping school leavers find work as early as 1890 (Milsted 1960).

All this had grown from the intense interest in social progress in the latter half of the nineteenth century, and a realisation that the labour market was not working well. Intervention could promote mobility and reduce under-employment to the benefit of individuals, employers and the economy as a whole. Education could play its part by widening and increasing aspiration, providing the skilled labour so necessary to the new industries in this new century.

There was no central policy objective. The impetus came from educationalists, social workers, charities and employers, all concerned about the problems caused by chaotic entry to employment and consequent waste of talent. There was a macro-economic dimension: a general acknowledgement by classical economists that intervention was necessary to make the labour market work efficiently. R.H. Tawney wrote that the nation's principal asset – juvenile labour – was wasting away. William Beveridge argued that decasualisation of labour was necessary to forestall economic depressions.

Government found itself responding to the national conscience and a general awareness that industrial change had happened without regulation. There was a need to catch up. Entry to work could no longer be governed by tradition alone: vocational guidance was a response to industrialisation and urbanisation.

The twentieth century was to follow the pattern noted by Lord Melchett when reviewing the progress of educational and social reform in the nineteenth century. Speaking at a conference on unemployment in 1911 he said: 'It looked as though each generation in turn gathered force to carry forward the movement which their predecessors had begun' (NAJEWO 1928).

From its beginning in about 1902 the development of career guidance and employment services for young people followed 20-year cycles up to 1995: each generation building upon the achievement and experience of the last.

This book sets out to chronicle a century of the service created to help young people choose a pathway through life, described variously in terms of employment, occupation or career. The intention is to consider the problems faced by policy-makers and practitioners, examine the solutions they adopted and draw conclusions which might help to provide a basis for future policy.

Chapter 1

1902–1948 juvenile employment and welfare

Work that is essentially educational

The year 1902 marks the end of the Victorian era and the beginning of a new age of public and social administration which, of course, includes the provision of career advice. From the beginning there were separate approaches. Herbert Heginbotham, *The Youth Employment Service* (1951) describes the 'educational side' of the argument for an official body to advise young people about employment, gathering strength from the 1902 Education Act and the education authorities which replaced the Victorian School Boards. This was different from the approach of the influential individuals and associations who had originally set up the first 'registers'. Working within the traditions of Victorian paternalism they had expected to continue to advise young people directly. Staff, where they were employed, were to perform clerical work rather than interview and advise.

But 1902 was also a significant year for an alternative approach to finding appropriate jobs for young people. The Labour Bureaux (London) Act was passed, marking progress within the labour exchange movement. Here again the impetus had come originally from the voluntary tradition through agencies set up on a philanthropic basis to help unemployed men find jobs. The first was the Egham Free Registry, established in 1885. William Booth, the founder of the Salvation Army, opened several 'labour registries' in 1890. He included waiting rooms with tables where registrants could write applications for jobs. Brian Showler in *The Public Employment Service* (Showler 1976) records that there were 25 public labour bureaux and 17 private bureaux operating nationally in 1893. The ten operating in London were administered by the local authority until 1899 when it was realised that expenditure for this purpose was *ultra vires* (illegal). The 1902 legislation recognised their value by putting them on a firm statutory basis.

Local authorities outside London were later empowered to follow this lead, through the Unemployment Workmen's Act 1905: few did so however. William Beveridge, the leading exponent of labour exchanges, was so convinced of the value of a national network that he influenced Winston Churchill, President of the Board of Trade, who consequently introduced the Labour Exchanges Bill, which would become law in 1909. While principally designed for use by adults, labour exchanges would also place young people in jobs.

Churchill's reputation as a social reformer has suffered at the hands of some historians but his early vision was extraordinary. Roy Jenkins in *Churchill* (2001: 147) records his letter to Asquith in 1908 when he called for:

1   Labour Exchanges and Unemployment Insurance;
2   National Infirmity Insurance, etc.;
3   Special Expansive State Industries – afforestation, roads;
4   Modernised Poor Law;
5   Railway amalgamation with state control and guarantee;
6   Education compulsory till 17.

There was, however, a general suspicion of the Board of Trade amongst educationalists. Industrialists and employers in general were still seen as the exploiters of workers, especially young workers, a prevalent view in the previous century. The Board was seen as representative of employers, opposed to the continuation of education beyond school and against the raising of the school-leaving age which was then 14 (or 13 in some cases).

The debates on this Bill did much to stimulate the interest of education committees, teachers and voluntary workers in the problems of school leavers and their entry to employment. Gerrold Milsted (Milsted 1960) remembered MPs taking the view that greater efforts to help young people would eventually have the effect of reducing adult unemployment. He was sceptical of Churchill's assurances that labour exchanges would take special care in the placing of juveniles, setting up advisory committees including representatives of education to oversee the quality of work. Churchill maintained, however, that there was no intention of placing upon labour exchanges the primary responsibility for placing young people in employment: he foresaw a co-operative arrangement with education authorities.

A pamphlet unearthed by Harry Foster of Derbyshire (1965), 'The Derby Labourers Hire 1903' commented on the difficulty faced by headteachers in interesting parents in school leavers' choice of worthwhile work and called for the appointment of one official for each town who would visit all schools, convince some parents to lengthen the period of schooling, advise on the best openings and influence some to enter technical training: 'For less than £200 per year a fatherly supervision might be exercised that may save many a one from shipwreck and disaster.' Heginbotham (1951) points out that the movement towards an official organisation to advise young people about employment had been growing steadily in the period from 1902–1909. In 1904 Mrs Ogilvie Gordon produced a detailed scheme for 'Educational Information and Employment Bureaux' for young people to be opened throughout the United Kingdom. Each bureau was to be controlled by a joint committee of members of the Education Committee and representatives of Chambers of Commerce, Trades Councils and other interested bodies. The aims of the bureaux would be to lead individual boys and girls towards employment which they would find congenial and financially rewarding and, at a more general level, promote closer co-operation between schools and employers.

Each bureau was to be administered as part of education. The 'Director of the Bureau' was to interview and advise children and their parents, keep in touch with the requirements of employers, keep records and work closely with evening institutes and voluntary bodies.

This scheme was submitted to the President of the Board of Education and the Secretary of State for Scotland with strong support from teachers' associations and trade unions. Edinburgh, Nottingham and Cambridge were among the first to take practical steps to put it into practice.

Meanwhile, the Labour Exchanges Act had become law in 1909 with its own proposals for helping young people. The Board of Education was not satisfied with these arrangements however and introduced the Education (Choice of Employment) Bill. During the debate on this bill Winston Churchill made it clear that he envisaged a system where in some areas the service to young people would be, in Heginbotham's words, 'more in the hands of the Labour Exchange and in others more in the hands of the Education Authority' (1951).

The Education (Choice of Employment) Act (1910) subsequently gave power to local education authorities (normally county councils and county borough councils) to make arrangements, with the approval of the Board of Education, to give assistance in choosing employment to children up to the age of 17. This would involve the collection of information and the giving of information and advice. Similar powers had been given to School Boards in Scotland in 1908. A subsequent joint memorandum from the Boards of Education and Trade urged education authorities to take up their powers and submit 'model schemes' for approval. And so through separate legislation passed in successive years responsibility was divided. The two departments concerned then made an arrangement that in areas where education authorities had taken responsibility they should interview, advise and register juveniles. The labour exchange would register vacancies, place juveniles in work and review their progress.

The practical issues arising from divided responsibility soon became apparent despite a joint memorandum from the Boards of Education and Trade requiring co-operation. Arrangements would vary from area to area. Officers of the education authority and the labour exchange would be expected to co-operate, working sometimes in the same office, but would have different responsibilities. One would be responsible for giving advice, the other for placing in work. The joint memorandum itself laid down procedures to be used in the event of a difference of opinion. As Heginbotham points out:

> Under this system a boy who wanted to be a clerk might be advised by the Education Officer to wait for a special vacancy, but calling in the next room for placing, another type of vacancy might be offered. Returning to the Education Officer he might be advised to refuse the vacancy offered.
>
> (Heginbotham 1951: 44)

Despite the awkward administrative framework within which they worked, individual officers were soon engrossed in their tasks. Gerrold Milsted remembers that he and his 'Board of Trade Co-operating Officer' agreed that their first loyalty was to the boys and girls they worked for. Working to improve their life chances for them must have seemed straightforward. The approach certainly wasn't value-free. Leaflets issued by the Edinburgh School Board provide a good example. 'Thoughts for a Boy on Choosing Work' (Smith 1911) gives clear instructions:

- Learn a trade if you get the chance.
- Learn to work with your hands – that will make your brain strong.
- Stick to your school 'til the last possible moment.
- Remember that you can receive instruction at day continuation schools.

'Thoughts for a Girl Choosing Work' is similarly blunt:

- Choose healthy work.
- Be brave and cheerful in whatever you choose to do.

But both leaflets are clear about the essentials: the importance of careful decision-making, involving parent and teachers and, perhaps most important of all, to young people unused to receiving help, the address of the office (open late on one evening each week) where they could get advice on changing jobs. To many who might previously have known only about casual jobs passed on by friends or family this would be a great step forward.

Before any substantial progress could be made the 1914 war began. The few juvenile employment bureaux which had opened became little more than registration offices for young people entering munitions factories and other essential but often repetitive war work, usually involving little training or choice. By-laws were relaxed and many children left school early. Heginbotham reports that their morale fell and juvenile delinquency increased. But the war seemed to focus attention on a range of social issues. Among these was the need for better arrangements to improve the transition from school to work and deal with the overlap between the Boards of Trade and Education.

The context of 'choice of employment work' was changing. Theories of vocational guidance were emerging. Elton Mayo and F.W. Taylor were applying industrial psychology to personnel selection. Cyril Burt, appointed as a psychologist to the Education Department of the London County Council in 1913, was turning his attention to a study of psychological factors relevant to vocational guidance. Developments like these were to set the scene for major experiments in London and Birmingham in the 1920s, both involving the National Institute of Industrial Psychology, founded by C.S. Myers in 1921.

Within this broader context, developments were also taking place outwith the public employment services. Universities had traditionally relied upon their graduates entering a proscribed group of occupations, facilitated easily by personal and social contacts. By 1914, however, Cambridge and five other universities had set up appointments services. Nine more followed between the two world wars (Watts 1996). The example set by Cambridge directly influenced private schools. Headmasters and house masters had always been involved in giving advice but in the 1920s some set up appointments boards. Boys were taught to write letters and how to be interviewed before being submitted to employers. The Headmasters' Employment Committee, based in London, adopted another approach. Financed by the Ministry of Labour, it provided a placement service for boys from schools within a radius of about 50 miles of the city.

Meanwhile, practitioners in the mainstream public sector were reacting to developments in industrial psychology and elsewhere, and responding collectively to the needs of their clients. Juvenile employment officers were beginning to meet together as early as 1914 when many already believed that 'our raison d'être was to fight for the idea that the education and training of the adolescent was more important than finding him a job' (NAJEWO 1928).

The initiative taken in 1918 to form a 'Conference of Juvenile Employment Officers' was an acknowledgement of a common identity and the need to apply the use of professional expertise and theory to the needs of young people. This was to lead to the formation of the Association of Juvenile Employment and Welfare Officers in 1922.

By the end of the First World War in 1918 it was apparent that the administrative confusion left by the 1909 Labour Exchanges Act and the Education (Choice of Employment) Act was incapable of delivering a service sufficient to meet the needs of young people in the post-war period. A Ministry of Reconstruction report, 'Juvenile Employment During the War and After', revealed that the expected industrial transition would lead to widespread dismissal of young workers. Girls would be especially at risk as men returned from the forces. A new policy was necessary for dealing with juvenile employment overall.

One immediate response was to pass the Education Act 1918, which introduced a uniform school-leaving age of 14 throughout the county and raised the age limit for young people attending juvenile employment bureaux from 17 to 18. A departmental committee then recommended more financial aid to LEAs taking up their choice of employment powers.

But LEAs were becoming increasingly concerned about the attitude of the Ministry of Labour, which they accused of interference and outright competition. A letter from the Association of Education Committees to the Board of Education in 1919 described the competition between the arrangements set up by one government department with those of another as wasteful of funds and a public scandal. If the service was to be made efficient and effective the conflict must cease. Lord Chelmsford was therefore appointed to head an enquiry and make recommendations.

Chelmsford reported in 1921. He found that the 1911 arrangements, whereby LEAs were responsible for advice and labour exchanges responsible for placing in employment, were unworkable and should be abandoned. He believed there was no inherent reason why either the LEA or the Ministry should not carry out the work efficiently, but whichever was responsible should undertake the full range of duties including the payment of unemployment insurance, work for which LEAs should receive direct payment. LEAs should, therefore, be offered another opportunity to take up their choice of employment powers. The reorganisation which followed in 1922 meant that the great majority of county boroughs and most counties became responsible for choice of employment work. The dual system of administration remained but a workable compromise had been reached.

The question of central government responsibility still had to be resolved. The Committee on Education and Industry, under the chairmanship of Mr D.O. Malcolm, was asked therefore: 'To enquire into and advise upon the public systems of education in England and Wales in relation to the requirements of trade and industry, with particular reference to the adequacy of the arrangements for enabling young persons to enter into and retain suitable employment.'

The Malcolm Committee recommended that the dual responsibility for choice of employment work shared by the Board of Education and Ministry of Labour should be ended and that the Ministry of Labour should assume full responsibility. LEAs should, however, be given a free hand to develop their services individually as far as possible and the Ministry should set up a National Advisory Council for Juvenile Employment on which LEAs should be strongly represented. The government accepted these recommendations in March 1927. Responsibility was transferred to the Ministry of Labour in 1928. The Juvenile Employment Service had at last achieved sensible local working arrangements under unambiguous central direction.

The decade between 1918 and 1928 had seen a steady increase in the confidence, competence and influence of juvenile employment officers. The Association of Juvenile Employment and Welfare Officers had been influential in the debates on the Chelmsford and Malcolm reports and had urged the Association of Education Authorities to press their members to take up choice of employment powers and providing advice on a range of practical issues such as the payment of unemployment insurance benefits. The first volume of the Association's magazine issued in 1928 opens with a formal greeting from the Permanent Secretary of the Ministry of Labour, which in itself suggests strong official approval of the Association and its aims. Most of the articles and debates, however, reflect members' concern about the day to day issues affecting young people: welfare of children employed in the theatre; providing clothing for needy interviewees; farm training and apprenticeships.

The association soon forged a close relationship with the newly formed National Institute of Industrial Psychology (NIIP). Interest in psychometric testing amongst JEOs was extremely strong. Officers in Birmingham began their own research in 1925, immediately after the Chelmsford reforms had been put into operation. Impressed by the work of the NIIP in London schools, Birmingham LEA seconded two officers for training and then carried out a carefully controlled experiment to assess the value of testing in a number of schools. They subsequently trained a number of teachers and JEOs in testing and interpretation respectively. The results and their indications were then passed to JEOs for discussion with pupils and parents at the 'choice of employment conference' (careers interview).

Birmingham concluded that: 'The adoption of scientific methods in vocational guidance improves considerably the advice that can be given to children leaving school' and that: 'It is possible to give vocational guidance to all, providing trained teachers are available to apply psychological tests and JEOs are competent to interpret them' (Innes 1932: 64).

The increasing importance of the Juvenile Employment Service and the National Association of Juvenile Employment Officers continued during the period 1929 to 1939. The Association held two conferences each year and attracted speakers such as R.H. Tawney and the President of the Federation of British Industry.

The King and Queen visited the Cardiff bureaux in 1931. In 1937, conference was addressed by Ernest Bevin who was to become Minister of Labour, a member of the war cabinet and, later, Foreign Secretary. The advice of JEOs and their association was sought by Select Committees on the Shops Acts and by the Government when considering further education, industrial legislation and a variety of other employment topics. They were able to influence the age of entry to insurance which was subsequently lowered to include young people aged 15 by the Unemployment Act of 1936 (although its implementation was to be delayed by the outbreak of war in 1939 and postponed until after the war or 'for the duration', as it was often expressed.)

By no means all the work of the JEOs involved innovation. County Durham's *Handbook for the Use of Officers in Juvenile Employment Bureaux*, written in about 1936, gives a useful insight into their more routine work. Descriptions of the duties of the JEO and the 'Woman Officer' (work with boys and girls was largely confined to officers of the same sex) show the importance of unemployment insurance work and the amount of time and effort devoted to claims for benefit. The links between the officer in charge and headteachers together with the careful arrangements for inviting pupils and their parents to interviews in schools demonstrate how far the service had become part of the educational scene. Clear notes on employer visiting, vacancy filling and placing of young people 'in other districts' show systematic attention to the needs of young people and employers.

Other examples, taken at random from records held in Dundee and Warrington in the 1930s, reinforce the quality of occupational knowledge and information. Dundee's annual summary of local occupations for juveniles covered wages, holidays, training and promotion prospects for all except professional jobs (covered on a national basis) including hackle making, millinery, catchboy, fur trade and sock-making. An industrial visit report on a brewery in Warrington which would later be incorporated in a similar survey, criticises 'pig-headed and narrow-minded foremen' but notes that 'each 14 year old boy carries a manager's job in his luncheon basket'. Time spent on information gathering and vacancy finding was crucial in view of the employment situation nationally. In Sheffield in 1926, 33 per cent of boys leaving school worked as errand boys, 16 per cent of girls found work as general maids. In 1932 a 'school certificate boy' found work as a bottle-washer (Sheffield Education Committee 1951).

As the influence, experience and confidence of JEOs grew, so did their professional and academic interest in their work. The National Association first proposed instituting a formal qualification in 1935 and approached the University of London with a view to offering a diploma in Vocational Guidance. Discussions continued until 1939 when they became another casualty of the outbreak of war.

The outbreak of war declared on 3 September 1939, was quickly followed by a realisation that the mistakes of World War I must be avoided: young people must not be allowed to become 'unattached'. A number of steps were therefore taken to maintain some kind of order in youth employment and leisure activities.

The first step was taken on 27 November when the Board of Education announced that it would take responsibility for the welfare of young people, urging all LEAs to set up local youth committees. Youth service officers were appointed. This had an effect on the 'welfare' element of the JEOs' work. Many had been secretaries to the 'Joint Organisation Committees' which had co-ordinated youth activities since 1916 by virtue of their 'review of progress' of young workers which had always emphasised the inter-relation of work and leisure. The second step was for the defence regulations to require young people to register at juvenile employment bureaux, usually on Saturday mornings, with a view to joining youth organisations. Close co-operation between JEOs, youth workers and their committees became essential. In the meantime, the Ministry of Labour had taken a unilateral decision regarding the work of the Juvenile Employment Service, which led to direct confrontation with the NAJE and WO. The Ministry's decision was that in the areas for which it was itself responsible, all work in schools and specialist advisory work with young people would be suspended. The association, drawing on its own experience of the 1914–18, war decided to do all it could to keep JEOs in touch with one another during the war, providing a forum for the discussion and solution of common problems facing young people. It was decided to replace national conferences with regional meetings to avoid travel problems and to issue regular bulletins to keep members up to date with developments and new ways of working.

The first bulletin issued in January 1940 dealt with the extraordinary decision by the Ministry to abandon all school and advisory work with young people and to assume that LEAs would do likewise. Percival Smith, the president, who responded on behalf of the Association, wrote that the Ministry's decision 'makes one despair' (Smith 1940). He pointed out that the difficulties facing young people were serious enough to prompt a positive response of the Board of Education in seeking to meet their needs through their National Youth Committee. In particular he drew attention to the many boys and girls likely to leave school early, the evacuation of school children from many cities and the problems of transferring young people to areas with unfilled vacancies.

The Ministry of Labour 'was apparently the only Government Department which has not appreciated that the problems of adolescents have been increased by war conditions and must be tackled'.

LEAs carrying out choice of employment work did not suspend their services in the event but JEOs were horrified by the realisation that young people in those areas administered by the Ministry would be denied the service (they would of course be allowed to register at an exchange in the same way as an adult but this was clearly not good enough). To the JEOs young people were 'the nation's real capital' which must not be squandered, even in wartime.

Following a meeting between officers of the Association and officials of the Ministry of Labour and National Service, the Ministry issued a circular reinstating some advisory work with young people on the grounds that they might otherwise be attracted to unsuitable work during a period of labour shortage. School conferences and advisory work were resumed in employment exchange areas in May 1940.

The problems facing young people and their advisers were daunting. They included:

- The emergency regulations, which made it impossible to leave certain jobs without express permission.
- Evacuation of school children from one area to another.
- A surplus of vacancies in some areas and a shortage in others.
- The requirements of 'priority' employers which had to be met.
- The anxiety of some parents that a young person should get a job close to home regardless of suitability.
- Special problems facing older and able young people in the face of suspension of national recruitment examinations and the reluctance of employers to employ anyone close to the age at which they would be recruited to the armed services.

Even the lack of possession of a ration book could cause difficulties. The matron of the dormitory on Margaret Street in Birmingham reported that canal boat workers were making for the city, well known for its high welfare standards, and leaving their children at Margaret Street to be well cared for during the war. But they frequently sailed away down the canal without leaving their children's ration book. The matron, of course, could not buy food without the necessary coupons.

As the wartime arrangements settled down JEOs were able to do much to help their clients. A requirement that all vacancies for young people must be notified to the bureaux meant that the vacancy filling service improved markedly. National Service Officers who policed essential work orders (requiring workers to remain in certain jobs) were obliged to consult JEOs who could often ensure that a change of job in the interests of improved career prospects would be approved.

During the war years the quality of public administration and the efficiency of the bureaucracy, of which the Juvenile Employment Service was part, was extraordinarily high. The successful rationing of food is perhaps the best known example but the mobilisation of the armed forces, the supply of labour to vital industries and the maintenance of industrial relations by the Ministry of Labour were major achievements. Simply continuing to make services available to the public despite the loss of trained and experienced staff to the armed forces required dedication and improvisation. The Juvenile Employment Service was a good example of this.

But, as a result of working under pressure, much was learned about the management of public services and their rapid response to political priorities. Technical knowledge in fields like personnel selection increased as occupational psychologists like Alec Rodger, seconded to the Royal Navy with the tempo-rary rank of Vice-Admiral, put their theories and experience to the test. At a later stage, when resettlement of members of the armed forces began, the Army Education Corps gained valuable experience of preparing people for work. Harry Dowson, who was later a founder member of the National Association of Careers and Guidance Teachers, was one of several whose enthusiasm for careers education stemmed from participation in this process.

Even more remarkable was the way in which preparation for the post-war period began early in the war years. Heginbotham observed that articles on this topic began to appear in the educational press as early as 1940 (Heginbotham 1951). Arthur Greenwood, Minister without Portfolio responsible for reconstruction, appointed the Beveridge Committee in 1941, one of a number of Reconstruction Committees set up to prepare for a better world in which full employment and social security were to become household words. Sceptics might say that this was partly propaganda on the part of a war cabinet anxious to assure the population that the way of life they were fighting for would be better after the war. Even if this was so, it was indicative of a new social contract between government and governed.

As part of this process Ernest Bevin expressed his view that adolescents should not be employed for profit. The period up to the age of 18 should be devoted to school, further education and training. The 1944 White Paper on Employment Policy was to follow. Bevin, Minister of Labour in Churchill's War Cabinet and a Labour MP, formed an alliance with the Conservative R.A. Butler over the preparation of the 1944 (Butler) Education Act, one of its aims being an improvement in vocational education through day release up to the age of 18.

It was realised quite early in the reconstruction process that an efficient Youth Employment Service could make a substantial contribution to the new Britain. In October 1944 the Minister of Labour issued a memorandum on 'The Reconstruction of the Juvenile Employment Service' and invited a variety of bodies to attend a meeting to discuss the topic in November 1944. From this initiative grew the 'Committee on the Juvenile Employment Service' appointed in January 1945 under the chairmanship of the Ministry's Permanent Secretary, Sir Godfrey Ince. As part of this process Ernest Bevin remarked that 'The most important decision of a lifetime is the choice of a career or occupation.'

The committee was made up of representatives of education, local authorities, employers and employees in England and Wales and Scotland (but did not include a Juvenile Employment Officer). It held eleven meetings and reported promptly in November 1945. Their report is remarkable. Beautifully written, it remains an excellent example of official English: comprehensive yet succinct, detailed but objective. Heginbotham comments that it was regarded by some as a 'New Testament' but that to many JEOs it seemed rather conservative. It certainly raised immediate, widespread interest.

The committee was unanimous that dual administration could never be wholly satisfactory. The best way would be to have a system run by the same organisation throughout the country. That organisation could be the education authorities or the Ministry of Labour. But whatever organisation was chosen the service should be comprehensive. All young people should be interviewed, including those in selective and private schools. Teachers should be required to provide school reports or 'estimates' for all school leavers. Speaking at the vocational guidance conference of the National Institute for Industrial Psychology in 1945, Alec Rodger said the report would have been worthwhile for this requirement alone. He was right: this principle of involving teachers in career guidance from the outset laid the foundation of the partnership between advisor and teacher which was to prove so successful in future years.

In general, however, the strength of the Ince Report lay in the administrative structure it proposed. Its brief had been 'to consider the measures necessary to establish a comprehensive Juvenile Employment Service'. It did exactly that, producing a unique arrangement between two government departments, capable of meeting the needs of young people throughout the country. (Because that structure was embodied in the subsequent legislation it is described in detail in the next chapter.)

The acceptance of the Report in 1945 by the new, reforming Labour government and its subsequent implementation through experimental administrative measures in 1946 (when a central executive was set up) and in 1947 (when an advisory council was appointed prior to legislation in 1948) marks a watershed in the development of the career guidance service for young people. The importance it gave to providing high quality careers information and guidance, placing employment and review of progress as a necessary part of the welfare state, is an acknowledgement of the successful development of commitment, enthusiasm and growing expertise over 46 years.

Addressing the annual conference of the NAJEO in 1946, Sir Godfrey Ince gave this pledge on behalf of his Ministry: 'You will have the fullest co-operation in building and integrating a national service, forgetting the past and looking only to the future.' E.W. Woodhead, the Education Officer for Kent, who had been a prominent member of the committee, paid tribute to Ince and his impartiality. He discussed work with schools and employers and concluded, 'The workers in this field are more vital to its success than the scheme of administration' (NAJEWO 1946).

From the first efforts of the Conservative government to build on the efforts of voluntary bodies by permissive legislation in 1902 through the reforming Liberal Government's passing of separate acts in 1909 and 1910 leading to parallel approaches to the Juvenile Employment and Welfare Service (and a period of consolidation when 'the will to co-operate was not always present') the universal Youth Employment Service had eventually emerged via war-time reconstruction and the post-war Labour government. The three themes which have defined the history of career guidance services had also become apparent. They were and are:

- An uncertain administrative framework.
- A body of dedicated practitioners able to exert influence individually and collectively.
- Increasing awareness of the educational, social and economic value of career guidance as the twentieth century progressed.

Chapter 2

1948–1974 youth employment
Capacities, inclinations and opportunities

In 1948 the whole structure of the Welfare State was enacted, with legislation on national insurance, national assistance, industrial injuries and the National Health Service. Beveridge's five giants, 'Want, Disease, Ignorance, Squalor and Idleness', had been addressed. The initial stage of the process of reconstruction was complete.

Opinions vary on whether this was entirely due to changes brought about by the war itself, or the result of a more prolonged process of evolution beginning at the turn of the century, in 1902 or thereabouts.

In the case of the Youth Employment Service, created by the Employment and Training Act in 1948, it was probably the latter. The steadily growing belief that the natural corollary of money spent on education was the need to ensure that talent and attainment must not be wasted, together with the realisation that a modern economy needed the right people in the right jobs, led to the requirement to provide an identifiable service available throughout the country at the same standard.

The Employment and Training Act neatly encapsulates the educational, economic and social roles of the Youth Employment Service and its responsibility to the individual client, to employers and to society as a whole. The Minister of Labour and National Service was to provide:

> Such facilities and services as he considers expedient for the purpose of assisting persons to select, fit themselves for, obtain and retain employment suitable to their age and capacity, of assisting employers to obtain suitable employees, and generally for the purpose of promoting employment in accordance with the requirements of the community.

The Minister was to be responsible for the whole of the Service in Great Britain, whether local administration was in the hands of the local education authority (LEA) or his own offices. Despite the experience of the 1920s and 1930s when, to quote the Ince report, 'the will to co-operate had not always been present', the government had been unable to resolve the dilemma of the Ince Committee. Whilst the intention was that LEAs should normally provide the service, they would be required to opt in, leaving the Ministry to fill the gaps where they failed to do so.

The Act gave LEAs six months in which to decide whether they would submit a 'model scheme', containing details of the structure of the Youth Employment Committee they would appoint, the bureaux they would open and the staff they would appoint. They were required to undertake the service for the whole of their area, to co-operate with other areas and to administer unemployment benefit and national assistance for those aged under 18. The outcome was that 129 (of 163) LEAs exercised their powers under the Act, leaving 34 areas to be administered directly by the Ministry. Most of these were rural counties, for example, Northumberland, Shropshire, Devon and Cornwall.

The central administrative arrangement was clear and firm. The Minister's responsibility to Parliament for the whole Youth Employment Service was to be in the hands of a Central Youth Employment Executive, a unique form of co-operation between government departments. Chaired by an assistant secretary of the Ministry of Labour, the executive included four Principals; one from the Scottish Office, one from the Ministry of Education and two from the Ministry of Labour. (It isn't possible to equate these grades with those in the present structure but both were within the first division.) The Executive would have a locally based representative in each region.

The advisory arrangements under the Act consisted of a National Youth Employment Council, with members appointed to represent LEAs, teachers, employers and employees. The council had the power to appoint specialist committees and co-opt members with particular expertise. Committees for Wales and Scotland had chairs with places on the Council. There was no place for a youth employment officer on either the Council or the Executive. Even the inspectorate consisted entirely of civil servants.

The 'new' authorities preparing to run the service for the first time had to think quickly about the staff they would appoint. The Central Youth Employment Executive (CYEE) made temporary arrangements for them to work side by side with the Ministry's staff whom they would be replacing. The intention was to allow time to learn office organisation and procedures, and develop contact with local employers.

H.M.D. Parker, chairman of the Executive, addressing youth employment officers in May 1949, was careful to point out that appointment of staff was for local authorities to determine, and had some interesting views on the topic. He suggested there would be a place for university graduates, teachers interested in vocational guidance and local authority office staff. He hoped it would be possible to appoint some with experience in industrial training. Most important, he stressed personal qualities such as interest in young people, tolerance and patience, a good general education, and interest in education and industry. He pointed out that the voluntary nature of the service meant that, however sound the policy might be, it would be judged by the quality of the individual officer.

But what was the nature of the actual service to young people promised by the Youth Employment Service and what did the youth employment officers do? Catherine Avent (who was to be eventually appointed the first Inspector of Careers Education and a future President of the Institute of Careers Officers) wrote in 1997 of her early experience as an 'assistant youth employment officer' in 1949 when she first joined the London County Council's new Youth Employment Service (Avent 1997).

Her first job was to place girl school leavers in shops and offices. The emphasis was still that of the Juvenile Employment and Welfare Service: protecting young school leavers from entering work considered deleterious to their physical or moral welfare. Work in schools was limited to 'the school talk' given to groups of up to 90 pupils in school halls, and interviews, often held in the head's study. There the headteacher presided, flanked by form teacher, head of evening institute, youth worker and YEO. The 15-year-old school leaver was unlikely to make his or her own views clear under these circumstances but would probably do so later, alone with the YEO in the bureau. (The word 'bureau' caused problems initially: unfamiliar to most, it was pronounced variously as 'Buroo' or 'Brewery' in London and as 'Burene' in Sheffield.)

Jay Sadler (who later became the distinguished Careers Information Officer to the Inner London Education Authority in 1963) recalled that the West End Bureau in 1949 held no careers information other than a few information sheets from employers and a few 'Careers for Men and Women' leaflets designed for those leaving Her Majesty's Forces (Sadler 1997).

Everything was to change rapidly as YEOs recorded visits, helped develop and distribute the 'Choice of Careers Series' and, as in Catherine Avent's case, produce original research on professional entry qualifications and failure rates. But it was 1952 before YEOs in London were to fulfil their responsibilities to selective schools.

The 'school conference' style of interviewing took some time to die and eventually became superseded by the one-to-one interview. Unemployment benefit work in the bureaux became more routine, although its arcane rules and complex formulae still took a disproportionate share of the time of those appointed on their potential to work sympathetically with young people, rather than their ability to apply civil service systems.

More typical of the 'new' authorities was Sheffield, which issued its first annual report in 1950. The head of the old Ministry of Labour service was recruited directly from the local employment exchange with a salary equivalent to that of the head of a local secondary modern school, reporting directly to the Director of Education and his deputy. The staff were drawn from the LEA's welfare and administrative staff, experienced 'youth' staff from the employment exchange, returning officers from Her Majesty's forces, personnel staff from industry and the occasional young graduate.

A basic but effective service was rapidly put into place. All statutory school leavers received one 'school talk' and one interview. These were from 10 to 20 minutes in length and based on Alec Rodger's seven-point plan. Parents were invited to attend. Subsequent 'placing' interviews, introducing young people to employers' vacancies, were held in the Bureau, which was centrally sited and well used.

In 1955, 30,000 people used the Sheffield Bureau; 3,926 young people were placed in jobs. The progress of 5,930 young workers was reviewed, with 2,439 responding to the invitation to visit their youth employment officer on a Friday evening. Sixty per cent of parents attended interviews in schools. Two senior members of staff worked in most of the city's grammar schools. Careers evenings and conventions were held. The overall aim was 'to put before young people the opportunities that will enable them to develop satisfaction through accomplishment' (Sheffield Education Committee 1955–6).

There was no shortage of vacancies: so many employers were in need of young workers that it was frequently possible to find exactly what the individual young person was seeking. Advice included information on further education and leisure activities. Frequent job changing was the problem most often identified in the Bureau.

By 1955 Sheffield had not developed any specialism, although it worked in all secondary modern schools and in some selective and special schools. Liverpool, however, had a well-developed specialist service to disabled pupils. William Duncan, writing in *Occupational Psychology* in 1951, reported that a vocational guidance officer visited each special school at the time when the school medical officer was present. After a conference involving the medical officer, headteacher, parent and child, the vocational guidance officer made recommendations and, once they were agreed, set out to find suitable jobs. During 1951, 343 boys were placed in 71 different occupations and 236 girls were placed in 58 different occupations. This was a matter for congratulation as the received wisdom had previously been that disabled young people were capable only of work in a few, carefully defined jobs. The aim in Liverpool was to remove this stereotype (Duncan 1951).

These examples from London, Sheffield and Liverpool are taken at random to give a feel for the new service, but efforts to provide a recognisable national standard were implemented quickly throughout the country. One talk and one interview in school, followed by placing interviews and registration for national insurance in the bureau, followed after about six months by a review of progress interview at a specified evening session, was the basic entitlement. Although those who found difficulty getting or keeping a job became regular and sometimes frequent visitors.

The other unifying element in the service nationally was the adoption of a standard method of interviewing based on the work of Alec Rodger of the National Institute of Industrial Psychology (and later Professor of Occupational Psychology at Birkbeck College, London).

'The seven point plan' (Rodger 1968) was devised by Rodger for his own use while working on training plans for young offenders in Wormwood Scrubs prison in 1930. By the time it was published in 1952, it had been refined into a careful system for assessing jobs on the one hand and people on the other. It was designed for use in personnel selection and vocational guidance. Its universality was itself a strength.

The plan consisted of a series of questions which the adviser should ask about an individual, arranged under the following headings: physical make-up, attainments, general intelligence, special aptitudes, interests, disposition and circumstances. In defining the factors of career choice, Rodger would some-times reduce the essentials to three: capacities, inclinations and opportunities.

During the 1960s it became fashionable to talk disparagingly about 'talent-matching' and to regard the plan as mechanistic and limiting of individual ambition, when compared to subsequent 'developmental' theories. But in fact, Rodger's best used phrase was 'planned procrastination,' a neat description of how the individual could be helped to approach a decision point systematically, ensure that options were not being prematurely closed, and then postpone career choice until a further stage of vocational maturity had been reached.

Rodger was a gifted teacher and trainer, able to use words and systems in such a way that interviewing skills were available to many with a minimum of training and limited knowledge of the theory of career choice.

As the Youth Employment Service developed during the 1950s, training in the use of the seven point plan was made available to all experienced staff and new entrants. But the wider question of training was to mark a difference in the way the service administered by the LEA and that provided by the Ministry of Labour were to affect youth employment officers and their work. The National Youth Employment Council set up a committee to consider training for the Youth Employment Service in 1949 and recommended that training for new entrants should consist of a full-time course.

The Ministry of Labour decided, however, that its own youth employment officers should be trained by means of 'the Birkbeck course', six weeks of intensive training devised by Alec Rodger, taught by him and his assistant, Peter Cavanagh, helped by Ministry inspectors, based at Birkbeck College, London (the course was also made available temporarily to LEA youth employment officers unable to undertake full-time training). This approach fitted the wider pattern of training within the civil service, whose officers were regarded as generalists whose skills might be 'topped up' by extra in-service training as they moved from one field to another.

The local authority approach was quite different. There, the use of specialists was part of the fabric and many entrants, such as teachers and some social workers, trained before entry. Post-entry training and subsequent qualification were the rule. The Local Government Examination Board ran a variety of qualifications, and promotion was linked to formal qualifications in fields such as housing, public health, accountancy and administration.

This too was the approach favoured by youth employment officers. The first attempt to found a diploma in Vocational Guidance had been made in 1936, when the University of London had been approached. The National Association of Youth Employment Officers decided to launch their own diploma in 1947 and appointed an examinations board and a registrar. The first examination was held in 1950.

The first full-time training course began in 1948 when 19 students, drawn from teaching, social work, journalism and similar backgrounds, met at Lamorbey Park, Sidcup. Kent County Council and the University of Oxford Delegacy for Extra-mural Studies provided the Certificate. Professor Alec Rodger of Birkbeck College taught occupational psychology. This initiative was taken by the Youth Employment Officer for Kent, Ida Groves, who had foreseen the potential demand for trained staff as early as 1946.

Conditions of service were also different for youth employment officers in the LEA and the Ministry of Labour. The latter were career civil servants in the executive grade, liable to be transferred between jobs and centres according to the needs of their Ministry. Youth employment provided an attractive short-term placing for some ambitious, able officers wishing to widen their expertise but for most it was not a long-term proposition. Their career prospects lay in the employment exchange mainstream. Staffing was, therefore, a problem for the Ministry in the mainly rural areas in which it provided the service directly. Many of its experienced 'youth' staff had left to join the new LEA services; few of those remaining could afford to confine their careers to the Youth Employment Service.

There was a wider problem. The Ministry could not shed its employment and national service image. This was exemplified in an incident related by Ray

Hurst in his retiring address as honorary secretary of the Institute of Careers Officers in 1985. He told how, as a young national serviceman returning to civilian life in the early 1950s, he had registered for work and benefit at his local exchange. He had explained that as a successful young sergeant in the Pay Corps (but with no practical skills) he wished to find a job in an office offering good promotion prospects. The immediate response was that he must apply for a vacant machinist job the next day or his claim to benefit would be disallowed. He withdrew his claim and left to find his own job. Ironically, the one he chose was in the local youth employment bureau. The manager of the employment exchange was a member of the selection panel.

The reputation of employment exchanges – associated with compulsion, registration for National Service, signing for unemployment benefit and proving availability for work – did not sit easily in the minds of the public with an advisory service for young people. Many of the Ministry's Youth Employment Service staff were aware of this reputation, which they tried very hard to dispel.

The reputation of the Youth Employment Service overall was improving, however. The core of existing staff, strengthened by those who had returned from the armed services with a wider experience of life and often of management, was joined by a wide range of new recruits attracted by the prospects of working with young people in a new setting. Many had experience of teaching, social work or industrial training. Notable were the large number of able women, some attracted by the equal pay, a condition in local government but not at the time in teaching and the civil service.

There were problems; Heginbotham points out the difficulties caused by the short (often 3 increments only) APT (administrative, professional and technical) grades. As the service benefited from experienced personnel it consequently required longer grades, as in teaching. Some LEA staffing structures contained in the model schemes proved to be inadequate. Relationships with education department staffing structures were unduly rigid in some areas. But, despite this, the Youth Employment Service was emerging as an attractive career, offering training, prospects and high job satisfaction.

Education and employment were fields of intrinsic interest and at the centre of social and economic policy. An opportunity to work at the interface provided a valuable opportunity for those who believed that the quality of life could be improved through public service and by strengthening the hand of the next generation of workers, students and parents.

The 1950s are now often described as dull and grey. Richard Hoggart, looking back from 1959 when he published his best-seller, *The Uses of Literacy* (Hoggart 1959), described the cultural life of working people during the decade. While he feared for the future – threatened, as he saw it, by an increasingly popular but trivial mass media and a tendency to greater centralisation of government – he found much to admire. The forces of persuasion could be resisted. Ordinary people could withdraw consent. They were less concerned with material shortages. The new 'classless class' was freer than before.

Better housing, health services and schools improved the standard of living and promised even more for the future. There was some enthusiasm for what politics could achieve. For many the 1950s was a time of stability and satisfaction, with the promise of even better times to come.

Changes in decades rarely coincide with historical change but some differences in the work of the Youth Employment Service began to emerge in the early 1960s. The quality of YEOs' work had improved steadily throughout the 1950s but professional relationships with teachers had been slow to develop. This was largely due to the pattern of the teacher's working day and the way schools were managed.

Teachers had few 'free periods' in the 1950s. They stayed in their classrooms for the most part. The YEO's main contact with the school was with the head-teacher, who usually made arrangements for interviews, arranged for school reports to be available and sometimes took part in interviews. Contact with class teachers was incidental, at break times perhaps, or at the beginning or end of the school day. Some grammar (selective) schools had a 'careers master' or 'careers mistress' who would arrange for the YEO to interview potential fifth-form leavers but few were convinced of the value of vocational guidance to those who might go on to university.

Many teachers felt themselves excluded from the whole process. Most YEOs felt that their spasmodic relationship with schools was unsatisfactory: they believed that, given the opportunity, they could contribute to the broad ethos of the school community. Percy Walton, who became honorary secretary of the National Association of YEOs in 1960 described this in his 'Then and Now' paper in *Careers Journal*, the magazine of the Institute of Careers Officers, in 1981. He and many others were well aware of the impending changes in education and the parallel development of theories of careers guidance, which would support a more developmental approach (Walton 1981).

The main proponent of this approach was Donald Super, who had addressed the NAYEO conference for the first time in 1959. He took account of the work of Eli Ginsberg (an economist) who, in 1952, had described a process of occupational choice lasting about 10 years from the age of 11, consisting of 3 stages: 'fantasy,' 'tentative' and 'realistic'.

Super's theory was more complete. He described a process of growth, exploration, establishment, maintenance and decline throughout life. He talked of 'work as a way of life' and pointed out that people differ in their abilities, interests and personalities. Making choice is a continuous process, intimately linked with self-concept. This theory found immediate resonance among YEOs and fitted well with the wider changes in educational theory that were beginning to find expression in schools. Asking 'Who do I want to be?' rather than 'What do I want to do?' was seen to have direct relevance.

American influence and the rise of the counselling movement in Britain was also making a direct impact on careers advice in universities where appointments boards were beginning to evolve into institution-based Careers Services. Audrey Newsome, an experienced youth employment officer, set up the first 'appointments and counselling service' at Keele in 1963. Staff in other universities were influenced by this development and began to realise that offering information and advice was not enough. Guidance was becoming important (Watts 1996). In 1967 the Standing Conference of University Appointments Services was established, making it possible to view careers advice in higher education from a national perspective.

The Youth Employment Service and schools became the subject of discussion again in the mid-1960s. In 1964, the NAYEO journal *Youth Employment* devoted two whole issues to guidance in schools. In 1966, Peter Daws of the Vocational Guidance Research Unit at the University of Leeds wrote *A Good Start in Life* giving a British dimension to changing theories of career choice. As schools grew in size and responded to calls to extend education and introduce examinations of the Royal Society of Arts and similar bodies, YEOs took a seminal role in making pupils and parents aware of the practical advantages of extended education in terms of wider career choice.

In 1965, close co-operation between Youth Employment Service inspectors and Her Majesty's Inspector of Schools (who together inspected the Service) resulted in an imaginative national training scheme for teachers involved in careers education. Regional training teams of carefully chosen teachers, inspectors and YEOs led by staff inspectors, ran short residential courses throughout the country. Many LEAs complemented this initiative with training of their own. Careers associations were formed. Teachers began to think about forming their own national association. (The National Association of Careers Teachers was subsequently founded in 1969 at a conference sponsored by the Advisory Centre for Education in Cambridge.)

Youth employment officers found themselves much more welcome in sixth forms. Changes in higher education and an increasing awareness of the complexity of the choices facing abler and older school leavers led many schools to realise the value of having YEOs (often known as 'careers advisory officers' in selective schools) interview pupils in their sixth and seventh years. Co-operative working involving heads, sixth-form tutors and careers advisers increased.

The changes taking place so rapidly had become apparent to the National Youth Employment Council which, in 1964, set up a committee to 'define the main issues facing the Youth Employment Service in the light of recent developments in education and the changing needs of industry'. Chaired by the Countess of Albemarle, the membership of 11 included Gertrude Williams, the economist, and Alec Rodger. No youth employment officer was directly involved, however, except in giving evidence.

The recommendations of their 1965 report, 'The Future Development of the Youth Employment Service', acknowledged the progress made and set in train the development of the system of careers education and guidance that was to prove so successful during the next 30 years. In summary, their main recommendations were:

- Educational and careers guidance should be a team responsibility (of schools and the YES).
- Contacts with pupils should be earlier, more frequent and more extensive.
- Stronger links with further education.
- More specialist advice for older pupils and students.
- More contact with parents.
- Development of education–industry links.
- Specialists to deal with disabled young people.
- Wide improvements to careers information.
- Increases in staffing.
- Nationally approved salary scales.
- More clerical support.
- Recruitment of more women returning to work.
- A requirement to appoint only those who had completed a full-time diploma in vocational guidance course.

The report did not, however, recommend raising the age limit beyond 18, changing the name of the service, or propose uniformity in the administrative arrangements for providing the service locally.

Disappointment with the Albemarle Report was, therefore, almost inevitable. The high profile of the Chair, the genuine national interest in the topic (it was said to have produced the best attended press conference the Ministry of Labour had ever achieved), and the high expectations of the profession, invited disappointment. And this was the time of big reports, like Newsome and Robbins. Education was exciting and newsworthy.

Even allowing for the high expectations placed upon it, the report was pedestrian. The recommendations on salaries, training, research and so on were solid enough, but the big opportunities were missed. When questioned, Lady Albemarle was quite unable to defend the continuation of the dual system of administration, or to convince anyone that the requirement for LEA officers to undertake 12 months' training could be matched by three months' training for Ministry of Labour personnel.

A careful comparison between Ince and Albemarle by the editor of *Youth Employment* revealed that, in many ways, the former was more radical. There seems little doubt, for example, that Geoffrey Ince would have preferred a requirement for a report on every school leaver from every school, and no doubt at all that he would have seen an end to the system of dual administration of the service.

It is worth digressing at this point to look closely at the work of Peter Daws, whose book *A Good Start to Life* (Daws 1966) reflected the debate which followed the Albemarle Report and made its own significant contribution to theoretical and practical improvements in provision. Daws, then Head of the Vocational Guidance Research Unit at the University of Leeds, set out to provide a framework for the provision of vocational guidance and to define priorities, rather than attempt a technical analysis. He put the work of Alec Rodger, Donald Super and Carl Rogers into perspective and defined five principles on which a comprehensive guidance service should be based:

1   Guidance should aid a continuous process of vocational development.
2   In order to guide the client's vocational thinking, vocational counselling must involve much more than the provision of information and advice.
3   The aim of guidance is to help the client to understand and satisfy needs and values no less than to match capacities and attitudes.
4   Aftercare guidance for young workers and their employers is as important as pre-choice guidance.
5   These tasks can be properly undertaken only if made the responsibility of a team of complementary specialists.

Daws found that only three of these principles had been endorsed by Albemarle. He applauded the emphasis on co-operation and a team approach, but was concerned about the lack of emphasis on aftercare for early entrants to employment. He was intrigued by the report's use of the neologism 'occupational guidance', and noted that, within three months of publication, the Ministry of Labour had launched its own 'occupational guidance units'.

Alec Rodger came to similar conclusions. He accepted that the carefully timed announcement that the government would inaugurate an occupational guidance service seemed to spike the guns of those who argued for an age extension for the Youth Employment Service. He described this as 'accident or shrewd timing', and pointed out that ten times the resources were required if those failing university courses and adults changing careers were to be helped adequately. He and many others were uncomfortable about the lack of consultation, the exclusion of representatives of youth employment officers, and the very tight control exercised by 'the mandarins' (senior civil servants). He called for the inclusion of a youth employment officer in the National Youth Employment Council.

Rodger's reference to the new Occupational Guidance Service is indicative of wider developments taking place in the Employment Service at this time. Brian Showler, writing in the 1970s (Showler 1976), attributes these changing views to the National Plan for 1965 which, responding to an OECD conference report, acknowledged that the unemployment insurance function had become paramount. The objective was to move the Department towards becoming an economic agency predominantly about employment. This echoed Churchill's original intention when, in 1909, he had said, 'The exchanges are primarily agencies for dealing with employment rather than unemployment' (Showler 1976).

The occupational guidance units set up in selected areas comprised the first attempt to create a Careers Service for adults. Staffed often by ex-youth employment officers, they relied heavily on psychometric testing and sat rather uncomfortably in employment exchanges in the early years. Exchange staff tended to be sceptical about advice sometimes unrelated to placing in local vacancies. But within a wider perspective, their future expansion and the ongoing debate on the Youth Employment Service provide a fascinating example of career guidance as part of wider economic policy and set the scene for change in the 1970s.

The immediate result of the Albemarle Report, however, was to promote dissatisfaction and to postpone reform. In particular, it had failed to address the case for a wholly LEA Service and to acknowledge the legitimate need for professionals to be involved in the policy of the service in which they worked and were passionately interested. To their credit, however, the CYEE issued a memorandum implementing most of the Report's limited recommendations without delay in February 1967.

More generally indicative of the future was the address given to the 1966 conference of the Institute of Youth Employment Officers by the Junior Minister of Labour, Shirley Williams, whose reputation as a radical had provoked great expectations. Her talk raised some fascinating policy issues. For example, she referred to the probable future of employment patterns, the need for frequent skill changes, and the realisation that occupations would in future demand frequent retraining. She raised the question of whether there should be greater concentration by the Youth Employment Service on the needs of school leavers who failed to gain academic qualifications. She went on to welcome a recent DES publication on careers guidance in schools, recognised the progress made by YEOs and the part they could play in training and working with careers teachers.

She also acknowledged that developments in the YES had led to her taking a new look at the Employment Service. It is clear, with hindsight, that this was a 'departmental' speech, showing clearly the emerging policy of the Ministry. It dwelt upon the need for an employment service with an economic and social role, no longer concerned only with the unemployed, led by the occupational guidance units. There were clear warnings that the YES would do well to accept a restricted role within this exciting future: working in schools, but firmly based in the economic sector. The speech warned of the likely effect of the upcoming report of the Royal Commission on Local Government and foreshadowed the Department's introduction of job centres and the Manpower Services Commission.

Exactly one year later, in 1967, John Evenden, the Institute's President, took a close look at educational and employment policy and the place of careers work within it. Tracing the history from Winston Churchill's 1910 bill to provide vocational guidance for young people, and examining the economy of that time, he looked forward to a similarly complex but different future. Pointing out the rapid development towards a service economy led by growth and the application of electronics, he predicted an increase in the number of women and girls in the working population and warned against vocationalism in schools. He argued for 'planned procrastination' (Alec Rodger's phrase) and for more resources to help provide information and guidance to young people making career choices. On practical and administrative issues, he made firm recommendations based on 50 years of historical evidence: the service should be mandatory for all LEAs; external careers advisers should be available to all pupils and students; professional advisers should in future be known as Careers Officers. Later in 1967 the Institute's policy document, 'A Young Worker's Charter', complemented these proposals, setting out the rights of young people to preparation for employment, fair selection, induction, training and continuing education.

The government played for time, announcing that no decision on the future of the service would be made until after the report of the Royal Commission on Local Government had been received. But the debate was in full swing. Professor Lady Williams (Gertrude, the economist, not Shirley) called for a national all-age careers guidance service to be run by the Department of Employment. Stuart Towler, Youth Employment Officer for Coventry, wrote in support. Percy Walton, Honorary Secretary of the Institute, responded, dismissing their argument.

In January 1970 Lord Longford, the maverick but insightful chairman of the National Youth Employment Council, wrote to the Secretary of State for

Employment and Productivity with his report 'The Future Structure and Age Limit of the Youth Employment Service', expressing his own view and that of the majority of the Council, that the service should cover all young people up to the age of 22 and be mandatory upon all local education authorities. Many in education and elsewhere supported this view and were becoming more vocal. Development was all around: the National Association of Careers Teachers had recently been formed; Catherine Avent had been appointed the first careers education adviser in London. DES and DE co-operation in the training of careers teachers had impressed heads of schools and chief education officers. The potential of the careers officers' contribution to education as a whole was well understood and supported.

Rumour and tension grew. In early 1970, the Association of Chief Education Officers anticipated a possible take-over of the YES 'by stealth', and warned that it would 'stand and fight'. The CBI joined in the argument; the TUC renewed its interest. Careers advice had become topical and controversial: worth fighting over. The debate continued throughout 1970 as the new Conservative Government under Edward Heath was elected, determined to force Britain into a bigger, better and more efficient future. The economy was still buoyant; commodity prices were increasing. Britain was preparing to enter the Common Market in a search for stability in an uncertain world.

A need to improve the workforce was part of the vision. The Department of Employment issued a discussion paper, 'Training for the Future' in 1971. Education was to be the key. The James Report on the training of teachers took forward the debate. The school leaving age was to be raised. Local Government was to be made more efficient once the Royal Commission reported. While there was anxiety about unemployment reaching nearly one million after 25 years of virtually full employment, discussion ranged over the 'leisure society', the 'service economy', and the need to compete internationally. It was against this background and its effect on the everyday lives of their clients, that careers officers and those who worked with them became so focused on the future of their service and so frustrated by their constantly unfulfilled wish to do more.

Even the comparatively small service to independent schools was able to make progress. The Public Schools Appointments Board, which had seemed to be so threatened by the new Youth Employment Service in the 1950s, began to transform itself. An expansion, based largely on a package of test-based guidance purchased by parents, led to a wider range of membership of schools outside the Head Masters Conference, and of girls' schools. The Board was renamed the Independent Schools Careers Organisation in 1972 (Hicks 2001).

The development of the theory underpinning careers education and guidance stimulated more interest. While Peter Daws, Barry Hopson and John Hayes discussed theories of vocational choice with Alec Rodger in a CYEE seminar within a largely 'psychological' framework, Ken Roberts published *From School to Work: A Study of the Youth Employment Service* (Roberts 1971) presenting a 'sociological' view of career guidance bounded by 'opportunity structures', which demanded a more practical response from careers officers. This intervention left careers officers with another factor to take into account, and sharpened the argument about whether career guidance was a service provided to individuals whose subsequent well-being might have a genuine beneficial effect on the economy, or whether it was, in Shirley Williams' phrase, an 'economic service', implying a heavy emphasis on people getting and keeping the right jobs so as to serve the national interest.

While the debate deepened and widened, including the supporters of an all age guidance service and those committed to a specialist, educationally based developmental approach in schools and colleges, the Department of Employment had been preparing its own policy initiative, *People and Jobs: A Modern Employment Service* (DE 1971), focusing on self-service, a professional and executive register, occupational guidance units, labour market intelligence and separation of job-seeking from unemployment benefit. It concentrated on the Employment Service. Little attention was paid to the YES, proposing that its duty to young people should cease after the first placing in employment and, inexplicably, that there should be a continuation of the universally derided split responsibility at local level, with LEAs allowed to opt in or out of their responsibilities, or sub-contract the service to the Department.

The reaction of careers officers was dismay. The word was used by Percy Walton, the Honorary Secretary of the Institute of Careers Officers. Ex-serviceman, graduate of the London School of Economics, sometime youth worker, practising careers adviser and writer on careers education and guidance, he typified the core strength of the profession and was to prove a formidable campaigner and political activist. Under his guidance, the Institute welcomed proposals for an improved employment service. (A 1969 survey of redundant workers had strengthened the general view that employment exchanges were 'a place for layabouts' and 'a place where you collect dole'.) Radical change was required. But, he argued, the limited role seen for the Youth Employment Service was insupportable.

The concern amongst careers officers was not that they would have less work to do. The intention of *People and Jobs* was that they should work amongst further education students of all ages, while their work in school ensured their continued security. It was ineptitude and ignorance that provoked their strong opposition. A paper concerned largely with the mechanics of job finding had casually disposed of career guidance in little more than two pages, without reference to theory, principle, practice or experience. Worst of all, perhaps, no account had been taken of 70 years of history when proposing an unworkable administrative structure, apparently designed to contain the Careers Service and define boundaries between it and the burgeoning employment service. The authors of the report, initially surprised by the strength of opposition, must have regretted the ambiguities, inconsistencies, poor staff work and inadequate drafting of this small section of an otherwise uncontroversial government document.

Reaction was strong and immediate. Neil Kinnock approached Percy Walton in May 1972 for a briefing which would allow him to raise questions during a debate on a related initiative, 'Training for the Future'. Kinnock was instrumental in reinstating the Labour Party's Employment Group, with Barbara Castle as a member and Reg Prentice in place of Jim Callaghan. Lobbying began in earnest.

Dudley Smith, the Department of Employment's Parliamentary Secretary of State, commented on the size of his postbag when he addressed the Institute's annual conference in September 1972. While he felt unable to make an announcement on the future of the service, he hinted that the universal view amongst local authority associations that the service should be mandatory would prevail. He emphasised the need to strengthen staffing and to consider mandatory training for careers officers. His references to the problems of Ugandan Asian young people, youth employment and new initiatives like 'Community Industry', also suggested that he was well aware of the need for a strong, secure Careers Service if government policy was to work as it should. In December 1972, the government produced 'Into Action – A Plan for a Modern Employment Service'. The policy, which would result in the Manpower Services Commission, was rapidly taking place. No proposal for the future of the YES was included, however. The strength of opposition to the government proposals appeared to be having an effect.

The campaign went on relentlessly. Even Harold Macmillan's announcement of the formation of a Manpower Services Commission on 22 November 1972 was met immediately by a question from the opposition spokesman, Reg Prentice, on the future of the YES. Macmillan's reply that an announcement would be made 'before too long' provoked anger amongst local authority representatives, teachers and careers officers. Seven years after the Albemarle Report, the problem was still not resolved. Ken Cooper, appointed to head the Employment Services Division, unused to dealing with education and local authorities, made matters worse by careless responses to approaches from the local authorities associations.

The strength of feeling and influence of careers officers had taken ministers and civil servants by surprise. It was said that the Permanent Secretary would not have Percy Walton's name mentioned in his presence. John Evenden of

Croydon became well known in the House of Commons tea-room, provoking parliamentary questions and hardening opposition wherever he could. Alice Thomas of Brecon, little known outside her area, was sufficiently influential in Wales to summon all South Wales MPs to a tea party and leave them in no doubt about the strength of feeling in the Principality. The strong local base of the YES was ensuring that almost every MP and every local authority leader was well aware of the importance of career advice to the young people in their constituencies.

The introduction of the Employment and Training Bill to the Commons in March 1973 intensified the lobbying. The NUT, the LEAs and the Institute united in the belief that the new service should be mandatory upon LEAs, should be staffed by trained careers officers and should deal with all young people, preferably up to the age of 21. Support grew from MPs and members of the House of Lords, across party, especially as it became apparent that the government's procrastination was due to a concern 'not to cripple the MSC' by 'excluding' young people from job centres.

The Institute's efforts, now led by Ray Hurst as Honorary Secretary and Percy Walton as Vice President, persisted throughout the Committee stage and the House of Lords. Even after the announcement of the government's broad intention to make mandatory on LEAs the provision of a guidance service for those in education, Percy Walton demanded further clarification of the role of the MSC, the period during which transitional arrangements would apply and the nature of the service to the young worker.

The constant questioning was well justified. The Employment and Training Act, when published, was clear enough in its main aims but ambiguous in its provisions for students in part-time education, those leaving higher education and the arrangements for young workers. It gave the impression that the Department was reluctant to see LEA involvement with anyone who had left education and loath to limit the new MSC in any way.

Nevertheless, the government's final intentions to locate the Careers Service in education were clear. The mandatory duties to provide vocational guidance and placing for school leavers were placed firmly on LEAs. The additional powers remained imprecise, but at least allowed LEAs to provide services for those who had left education and for adults, providing they could find resources to do so. But the phrase 'it is not the intention of the Act that authorities should attempt to provide an all-age service', seemed to demonstrate the Department's reluctance to accept the full potential of career advice to life-long learning.

The three themes (an uncertain administrative framework, a body of dedicated practitioners and increasing awareness of the value of career guidance) which had become apparent in 1948 had persisted throughout the 20 years or so since the end of the Second World War.

The administrative framework had become progressively more uncertain since 1948 and a matter of dispute during the 1960s. An attempt by central government to end uncertainty had been rejected by local interests. But the essential compromise explicit in the 1973 Act: a service locally administered through education, retaining central responsibility through the Department of Employment, appeared to provide a sound basis for future development.

The strength of the body of dedicated practitioners had proved decisive. By demonstrating their commitment and ability to defend their ideals, they had secured their right to influence the future of the service within which they operated.

Their success was partly due to the third theme: awareness of the educational, social and economic value of career guidance had continued to grow throughout the period.

In 1974, the prospects were bright. A firmer administrative base, a strong body of practitioners and ever growing interest in the work promised much for those who were to use the new Careers Service, those who would work within it and the governments whose policies it would put into practice.

Chapter 3

1974–1994 careers

A progress through life

The process of legislation had been exhausting but exhaustive: none of those who had taken part could feel that their views had been ignored. The Employment and Training Act marked the moment of transition from the Youth Employment Service to a Careers Service, mandatory upon all local education authorities: a public acknowledgement of the beliefs held by the early juvenile employment officers. The work of helping young people to choose careers was essentially part of the educational process. There was a general sense of relief, a great deal of enthusiasm for the wider remit and the opportunity to concentrate on providing a much improved service.

Reaction at the Department of Employment was interesting. The most senior civil servants felt they had lost ground: their original grand design had been rendered incomplete. Their major concern, therefore, was with the Manpower Services Commission and more especially its Employment Services Agency: nothing should be allowed to stand in the way of success. Every potential client should be encouraged to use its very expensive job centres. The flavour of their position makes itself felt in *The Careers Service: Guidance to LEAs in England and Wales*, the publication which set out the way in which the Act should operate at local level. Even there, stress was placed on the responsibility of the MSC and its executive arms (the Employment Services Agency and the Training Services Agency) over the whole field of employment. Their involvement with the 16–18 group post-education is also emphasised. LEAs, on the other hand, were reminded that while they were not excluded from working with adults, providing they could find the resources to do so, it was not the intention that they should attempt to provide an all-age service.

The senior civil servants were themselves undergoing transition of course, learning to see themselves as paymasters rather than providers; preparing to distance themselves from direct management. The Act's withdrawal of a specific grant implied a wider withdrawal from the Careers Service in its LEA setting. But it soon became apparent to those directly responsible (who had made up the CYEE previously) that principal careers officers believed their partnership with the Department should continue, albeit in a different form. Active co-operation with the centre and its regional representatives should continue.

The Department's duty to ease the transition process in areas providing the service for the first time was carried out generously. The LEAs had adequate opportunity to house and staff their new services before DE staff were withdrawn. Goodwill at local level was further strengthened by the absorption of careers officer civil servants who wished to join the new Careers Services. Only a few chose to do so (career prospects on the whole were not so good as in the civil service), but their welcome, despite a restrictive local government union policy, was an important gesture of goodwill. The transition at local level was handled well.

Reaction by local authorities and their associations was predictable. They felt themselves vindicated by the provisions of the new Act. Local government reorganisation which had taken place simultaneously had also released tension. There was a feeling that local authorities had been incomplete without an employment arm. Chief education officers whose authorities had not run their own Careers Services had felt the lack keenly. They set about their task with enthusiasm. Local innovation became a feature of the new services. Wiltshire, for example, espoused close integration with schools and a strong emphasis on locally produced careers information. They appointed a principal careers officer who shared these views and a deputy who had worked as a careers teacher. Shropshire placed its principal careers officer close to the advisory service with a deputy who would manage employment work.

The enthusiasm of the 'new authorities' was to be tested, however. The international oil crisis of 1973/4 caused problems in both public and private sectors. Such essentials as office furniture, printed paper and telephone systems were difficult to buy. Constraints on local government expenditure made the acquisition of premises difficult and affected staffing ratios; the predicted shortage of trained staff made recruitment difficult. Energy had to be directed to maintaining a basic service to pupils in schools, students in colleges and young unemployed people. Innovation, improvement and expansion had to wait.

The most fundamental change as a result of the new Act was upon the staff of the service and their view of themselves. They had been strengthened by the process of change as well as by the legislation itself.

While much of the debate which led to the Act had been ostensibly about administrative arrangements, the underlying questions were about professionalism and the environment in which it might flourish. Many careers officers had realised that they would have higher salaries and greater career prospects within the Manpower Services Commission (the Chief Inspector himself had leaked information about proposed higher salaries). Rumours had persisted that a major reason for the Department's wish to take over the service had been the acquisition of 3,000 qualified careers officers of graduate calibre to strengthen the cadre of the MSC. But careers officers had voted firmly for a place in education and a chance to become far more influential in schools, colleges and education committees. The opportunity to practise career guidance in this setting was taken with enthusiasm. An all-age guidance service based in LEAs became the long-term aim of many despite the ambiguities of the Department's guidance.

There was greater confidence also in the technical competence of careers officers. Nicola Cherry's work for the Medical Research Council at the London School of Economics confirmed that young people who followed careers officers' advice stayed longer in their chosen jobs than did those who took up alternative work. This was due largely to accurate assessment of abilities and interests by careers officers, rather than to other factors, she believed (Cherry 1974).

Respect for the contribution of careers officers to schools continued to increase. Headteachers took more interest. The National Association of Careers and Guidance Teachers grew stronger and widened its contribution to in-service training. Discussion on who should do what and the nature of the careers officer/teacher partnership developed throughout 1974. An examination of the process of vocational guidance emerged, proceeding through orientation, information, assessment, planning, adjustment and readjustment where necessary. The contribution of teachers and careers officers was seen as complementary. Teachers worked within careers education, information and orientation: careers officers specialised in guidance, assessment, placing and adjustment (Peck 1975).

By the end of 1975, it was possible to look back on a period of solid achievement. Faced with the general economies they had been forced to make from 1973, the LEAs could have been forgiven for economising on this new responsibility. In fact, the number of careers officers had increased not just absolutely but proportionately to the number of pupils reaching school-leaving age. The young person was seen universally as the primary client, with the interest of educational institutions and employers seen as important but secondary. By providing statistical information, feedback and opinion, Careers Services were found to have an additional value to LEAs. The Employment and Training Act was living up to expectations (Peck 1975).

There was to be little time for further consolidation, however. Unemployment and its consequences for young people were having an accelerating effect on the service. The shortage of opportunities for young people was exacerbated by an increase in the number of women entering the workforce, a decrease in the population of men reaching retirement age and, most important of all, the 'bulge' in the number of school leavers (Bradley 1990). The school leaver cadre in 1969–70 had been 691,000: by 1975–6 this had grown to 817,000. (This growth was to continue until 1982–3 when it reached 913,000.)

This formed the backdrop of the 1975 Institute of Careers Officers' Conference where the President, Percy Walton, spoke on 'People with Problems' describing an age of discontinuity. Ray Hurst warned that the level of unemployment tolerable to society was steadily rising with grave effects on young people. There was discussion of 'Community Industry', a voluntary sector organisation set up to provide placements for unemployed young people, working closely with careers officers. And there was anxiety about the failure of the MSC to take account of the knowledge and expertise of careers officers when forging policy.

This anxiety about the Manpower Services Commission proved to be well justified. Ken Cooper, the Employment Service Agency's (ESA) Chief Executive, declared his general position at about the same time. Describing the Agency's two groups of clients – employers and job seekers, he placed first the responsibility to fill vacancies and pointed out that, as a consumer service, 'the Agency would wish to see as many people as possible benefit from what was on offer'. He described the Occupational Guidance Units' success in increasing market share, stressing the fact that 60 per cent of its 50,000 clients were under 25 and many more entering their first job. He welcomed the opportunity presented to the Agency by the Act's provision to abolish the age limit of 18 for young job seekers, and announced the appointment of employment advisers with special responsibilities for dealing with young job seekers in anticipation of demand. He also reinforced the occupational guidance services on the same grounds. His subsequent call for closer co-operation between job centre managers and Careers Services rang rather hollow after that announcement.

Careers officers had seen the future rather differently. The opportunity for young workers to use job centres had been seen by the government as a civil rights issue. There seemed no doubt, however, that the great majority of young people would be best served by revisiting the careers adviser who had seen them at school and helped them find their first job. The idea of competition between job centre and careers office seemed to run contrary to the intentions of the 1973 Act and the wishes of government. Occupational guidance units presented a more complex issue. Created in 1966 to provide help for those who had made a false start or were looking for new opportunities, they had been seen as the Careers Service for older workers. Now, as the third tier of the job centre, they were well placed to meet a potential growth in demand from those displaced by industrial change or wishing to find wider opportunities to use acquired skills. There were doubts, however, about their ability to deal with young graduates and first-time job seekers. There was concern too about the ability of career civil servants seconded to give careers advice on the basis of short in-service training to match the professional expertise available from careers advisers.

Careers advisers had welcomed the ESA and its improved service to employers, its enhanced facilities for the jobless, its self-service style and its high street premises. It had a philosophy very different from the client-centred position of the Careers Service, however. That the two should be complementary seemed to be in the interest of all; that they should compete seemed wasteful and destructive. Careers Services knew they should not compete and never intended to do so. Many wished, however, to offer a selective service to adults and found themselves almost obliged to do so. Many young graduates, women returners, late qualifiers and others demanded help and turned naturally to their local careers adviser whom they remembered from school or, in the case of older clients, had seen work with their own sons and daughters.

The ESA's chief executive's statement was seen, therefore, as an extravagant and unhelpful challenge on behalf of a Manpower Services Commission anxious to dominate and exclude others, an early sign of the Balkanisation which Geoffrey Holland was later to deplore. But while the behaviour of some people in the MSC produced some irritation, careers officers were not distracted from their work. Day-to-day demands grew steadily. Four main elements dominated the work of the Service from 1975 to 1979:

- Measures to contain youth unemployment and the need to make them work to the advantage of individual young people.
- A need to change emphasis to meet the needs of young workers (applying the lessons learned from Ken Roberts and his 'sociological' view of careers guidance) (Roberts 1975).
- Taking part in a campaign to improve careers education and the way pupils prepare for working life, as a result of the Prime Minister's 'Ruskin speech' in 1976 and the 'great debate' on education which ensued.
- Meeting the needs of adults who approached careers offices for help in changing careers and re-entering a complex and difficult employment market.

This agenda kept the service at the centre of public policy-making; constant development ensured a stimulating and challenging environment in which to work. Ray Hurst, the Honorary Secretary of ICO, was able to point out in 1977 that: 'Never has so much been written about vocational guidance techniques,' and 'The quality of recruits to the Service has never been higher' (Hurst 1977).

He went on, however, to link the greater recognition achieved by the Careers Service to a need to concentrate on the employment role and the needs of young workers for help in improving their career prospects. This reflected also the continuing debate on the application of the established 'psychological' or developmental theories on choice of career and the recently increased emphasis on finding the right opportunities for school leavers – the 'sociological' view.

The so-called 'talent matching', or 'trait and factor analysis', typified in the minds of many inexperienced careers advisers by the work of Alec Rodger, had been unfashionable for some time. But Rodger had identified three determinants of career choice – capacities, inclinations and opportunities, allowing for a developmental approach within a practical framework (Rodger 1968). Ken Roberts' intervention had served to remind the service that 'opportunities' were crucial, especially to young school leavers. The quality of this debate also increased the influence of the Careers Service on schools as teachers became more intrigued.

It was said that James Callaghan's concern for his grandchildren's education at a London comprehensive promoted him to speak his mind at Ruskin College in 1976, calling for the review of standards and the curriculum, which culminated in the Green Paper 'Education in Schools' of 1977. The 'great debate' which ensued began with regional conferences involving principal careers officers, chief education officers and headteachers and continued in every local education authority. The influence of the Careers Service as the bridge between school and work was strengthened as a result.

Interest in careers education and guidance remained high generally. In 1977, the Standing Conference of University Appointments Services transformed itself into the Association of Graduate Careers Advisory Services. The nature of university careers advisers was beginning to change as LEA careers officers were increasingly recruited (Watts 1996). The national investment in training for the Careers Service was beginning to produce dividends.

Much the most important influence on the service in the latter part of the decade, however, was the government's programme of special measures to combat youth unemployment, the part played in this by careers officers, (particularly the unemployment specialists who were recruited to help) and the constant need to ensure that nationally and locally the Youth Opportunities Programme allowed freedom of choice and matched the needs and abilities of the young people for whom it was designed.

The Youth Opportunities Programme was introduced in 1978 as a result of the 1977 'Holland Report', *Young People and Work* (MSC 1977). Geoffrey Holland, the outstanding civil servant of his generation, had brought together a committee whose members included Ray Hurst, honorary secretary of the

Institute of Careers Officers and principal careers officer for Cleveland. Hurst's practical experience, his careful phrasing ('persistent friendly cajoling' was one that stuck in Geoffrey Holland's mind) and his assiduous consultation with colleagues ensured that the expertise of the Careers Service was brought to bear on the programme. In that way, many potential errors were avoided.

YOP was inevitably criticised by the media and many trade unions as cheap labour and indifferent training. But it laid the basis and provided experience on which to base future policy: the Youth Training Scheme and the New Training Initiative were to follow. Geoffrey Holland was to apply the lessons learned during this apprenticeship to the benefit of the Callaghan, Thatcher and Major governments for the next decade and beyond.

The Institute of Careers Officers Conference of 1979 provided a good opportunity to take stock of the progress made since 1974 and to prepare for the next decade. The election of the Thatcher government had caused a great deal of apprehension in the public service generally and to some extent in the Careers Service. The extreme free market ideas of Hayek do not fit easily with careers guidance. In David Blunkett's words 'The doctrinaire libertarianism of Hayek and Friedman did not simply minimise government – it fostered a political discourse in which government activity was viewed as inherently inimical to public welfare' (Blunkett 2001). Careers Service relationships with the Callaghan government (especially with John Goulding the Minister of State at the Department of Employment) had been close and supportive. Even on the day before James Callaghan's resignation, and even during the debate in which the government was defeated, Goulding had been working on a requirement for LEAs to appoint only trained and qualified careers officers. Unfortunately he ran out of time. This was a fair measure of the importance he attached to the service.

There was a fear that those who operate in the 'soft' areas of education, like careers guidance, would not be popular with the new government, which was expected to advocate a free labour market. An early meeting with Lord Grey Gowrie, the junior minister directly responsible, did little to calm anxiety. The mantra with which he opened his first meeting with ICO officers was peppered with references to burdens on business and other tenets of monetarist economics. (Civil servants fared no better: Keith Joseph was said to have circulated Adam Smith's *Wealth of Nations* to his senior staff, but found that it was returned to him together with a Penguin paperback, *Teach Yourself Economics*.) So anxious was Gowrie to deliver his mantra that Desmond Burgess, the ICO Treasurer, had to remind him that introductions were necessary before the meeting proper could begin.

Relations with James Prior, the Secretary of State, were quite different. Meetings had been held with him whilst he was Shadow Employment Spokesman and ICO officers had prepared papers for him and for the Conservative Back Bench Education Group, chaired by Norman St John-Stevas. In his speech to the ICG September Conference, Prior stressed the vital role of the Service as it approached the 1980s. The Careers Service contribution to the YOP had been, and would remain, of great importance to its success. He emphasised that careers officers should expect a continuing substantial involvement in helping young people during the process of economic recovery.

John Goulding, another Conference speaker, was similarly congratulatory. From his vantage point as recently retired Minister of State, he pointed to the service's relative lack of confidence, and suggested it should become more vocal on policy matters, assuming the role of linking education and industry. Gordon Cunningham, representing the Association of County Councils, also stressed this developing function of the Careers Service. This became the theme of the conference.

The presidential address took the form of 'an appraisal of the structure with which the Careers Service operates, taking as the criteria the three elements used by Alec Rodger – how far can it claim to be technically sound, administratively convenient and politically defensible' (Rimmer 1979). The address went on to examine the relationship between the MSC, the Careers Service, local authorities and the Department of Employment. The role of the MSC should be to concentrate on its main functions as follows:

1   The prime function of providing central intelligence and manpower policy.
2   Establishing a strong regional structure capable of responding to national need.
3   Introducing coterminous boundaries and shared premises between its divisions.
4   Developing an improved service to less able job seekers.
5   Running regional and area boards, rather than District Manpower Committees.
6   Ensuring the appointment of a careers officer as a member of the Commission.

It should then withdraw from work that it could do less well than the Careers Service: occupational guidance for adults and employment advice to young people.

More radical was the prescription for the Department of Employment, responsible for both the Careers Service and the MSC. After supporting the existing position of the Careers Service with the Department of Employment rather than the DES, the address called for a more direct role for the Department and the strengthening of its Careers Service Branch. In particular, this should involve the re-grading of the head of Branch from assistant secretary to under secretary, and a new grade and status for Careers Service inspectors, in line with the position of HMI and inspectors of social services.

The grand vision was of a Careers Service branch responsible for the policy and quality standards of a pivotal Careers Service serving all in need of guidance, irrespective of age and working locally to ensure co-operation between industry and education, local authorities and the MSC within wider government policy objectives.

In the light of what was to happen in the 1980s, such an administrative base might have helped to mitigate the effects of unemployment and to assimilate the effects of the changing employment structure of the UK. It might have imposed some discipline on the MSC, making it more responsible, accountable and responsive. It would have helped to control the 'Balkanisation', which Geoffrey Holland ruefully acknowledged, and done something to mitigate the waste of public money which rivalry and duplication produced.

The Autumn 1979 Edition of *Careers Quarterly* reported the address fully. The editor, Avril Rimmer, commented, 'Within the context of the Annual Conference in which it was delivered, its impact was huge'. The message that 'we fail our clients if we devote ourselves so heavily to their welfare that we fail to look after their collective interests' was well taken by Institute members (Rimmer 1979). The scene was set for another great debate but it never took place. The politicians might well have been interested. James Prior's announcement to Conference that the new government had decided to retain the MSC, despite rumours that they would disband it, suggested initial doubts about its very wide remit. John Goulding's speech suggested that the opposition too would be supportive of the idea of a stronger, wider-based Careers Service. Local authorities were interested: articles appeared in the *County Councils Gazette*, *Municipal Review* and *Local Government Studies*. But the silence of the Department of Employment was deafening. The opportunity was missed.

Historical change rarely fits neatly into decades but 1979 marked a watershed in the story of the Careers Service, as it did in the history of the United Kingdom. This was the year of the Thatcher government and of Roy Jenkins' Dimbleby Lecture, which led to the foundation of the Social Democratic Party and, indirectly, to the New Labour movement and the 1997 Blair Government.

In his book *The Seventies*, Christopher Booker described the decade as 'Scarcely a time to cheer about, to quicken the pulse, to remember with excitement' (Booker 1979). Those who worked in the Careers Service had had a share of the limited excitement available and used the time to consolidate their position and improve their practice. But the 1980s were to be quite different. A government with a strong political philosophy, determined to revolutionise the economic and social structure of the nation, would provoke such rapid and fundamental change that a framework is necessary in order to be able to assess its particular effect on the Careers Service.

The three characteristics which had already begun to define the service in 1948 are again useful here. They are:

- An uncertain administrative framework.
- A body of dedicated practitioners, able to exert influence individually and collectively.
- Increasing awareness of the educational, social and economic value of career guidance as the twentieth century progressed.

In general terms, the administrative framework was to remain uncertain, partly because the opportunity to make it stronger had been missed but largely due to the exponential rise of the Manpower Services Commission and the relative decline of local education authorities. The body of practitioners remained influential but were too often placed in a reactive position as events achieved even greater momentum. But it was the increasing awareness of the value of career guidance, made more apparent by the pace of social and economic change, which was to dominate the 1980s and eventually dictate the future.

Local authorities retained their strong attachment to the Careers Service throughout the late 1970s and the 1980s but there were occasional difficulties which the government and the Manpower Services Commission found irritating. Entrusting the provision of national services to local authorities implies local determination of priorities. Some concern had arisen as early as 1975 about authorities who failed to spend the recommended amount of grant allocated to the Careers Service. The Local Authority Associations who had been so determined to be responsible for the service were, nevertheless, anxious to remind Whitehall of the independence of their members. Rate Support Grant, the means by which government money was allocated to local authorities, was unhypothecated: an important principle. As reductions in public expenditure continued through the 1970s and 1980s, each annual budget round involved hard bargaining and anxious times for principal careers officers. Local government provided opportunities for the political maverick. In 1978, Herbert Heginbotham, Principal Careers Officer for Birmingham, had made a dramatic announcement to the ICO Annual Conference that his council was considering asking the Department of Employment to run the Careers Service on its behalf so as to reduce local expenditure by the council. Whether this gesture was designed to remind the government that pressure on public expenditure could work both ways, or whether local rivalries played a part, is not certain but for Birmingham, which had pioneered psychological testing, and whose Chief Education Officer, Lionel Russel, had played a prominent part in building the Diploma in Careers Guidance, to behave in this way caused dismay throughout the UK.

In the event, the Department was able to point out that the Act did not allow for this procedure. The LEA was required to continue to provide the service. The atmosphere remained tense in Birmingham, however, until 1980, when Peter Jones was able to reassure individual members of the Council of the seminal role the service could play in the delivery of local policy.

A similarly maverick approach was later to be demonstrated in Leeds in 1984. The Leader of the Council put forward a proposal to radically change the management and operation of the service, basing all careers officers in youth centres and closing the central careers centre. It would have been quite possible to run the service and the youth services in tandem (Essex already did so quite successfully) but this proposal went further. Based on the belief that careers officers should concentrate on disadvantaged young people in disadvantaged areas, especially Seacroft, the outcome would have been the virtual withdrawal of the universal service.

Geoff Ford, the Principal Careers Officer, was put in an unenviable position. With no option but to oppose the plan, he was obliged to seek support from the regional office on one hand and the Institute of Careers Guidance on the other. Ironically, Geoffrey Holland, alarmed by the prospect of a withdrawal of the Careers Service from its central role in special measures, also played a supportive role. Leeds was prevented from having its way. Geoff Ford was removed to a post in adult education (from which he subsequently made a strong impact on careers advice for adults nationally), and was succeeded by Colin Thompson of Wolverhampton. This potentially important city never achieved its potential in Careers Service terms, however. The Leader of Leeds City Council at that time was George Moodie, who eventually inherited Denis Healey's seat in the Leeds constituency which includes Seacroft and subsequently became the junior minister at the DfEE at the time when the Connexions strategy was announced.

So, while the 1980s began with the Careers Service in good heart, confident in its ability to serve individuals, play a part in delivering national policy and contribute to the process of policy-making, the Service was always vulnerable to local difficulties. Some councillors, reflecting what they felt to be the Thatcher Government's philosophy of *laissez-faire* and minimal interference in business and the private lives of individuals, questioned the need to spend more money on careers education and guidance. Their argument ran like this: where there are jobs to be had, young people will find them for themselves; where there are no jobs there is no point in employing staff to advise on career choice.

A different but equally disturbing trend also began to appear among some teachers and youth workers, who argued that structural unemployment was now such that careers education and preparation for work was useless. Some young people would never find work and should, therefore, be helped to prepare for a life of leisure. 'Significant living without work' became a fashionable phrase.

The arguments deployed to rebut both these points of view were typified by a joint ICO/NACGT response in a COIC publication, *Careers Guidance in the 1980s* (Howden 1980):

> For the 1980s at least, our attitude to work as both intrinsically valuable for those who perform it and socially desirable to meet the needs of society, will persist. Leisure will remain the outcome of, rather than a replacement for, work.
>
> We must raise the level of attainment of the whole range of school leavers as far as possible so they may take advantage of the new jobs available and be less affected by the dearth of jobs for those with limited skills.
>
> We must continue to practise and improve careers education and guidance – the majority of young people will get jobs and all will be faced with adjusting themselves to the concept of a 'career' through life.

The government's strengthening of the Careers Service by additional unemployment specialist careers officer posts, and the 'Christmas Guarantee' ensuring that a young person leaving school should quickly be offered a place in work, further education or the Youth Opportunities Programme, demonstrated the practical advantages of this position.

The fundamental changes in employment and the need to involve schools and colleges in helping young people to prepare for it, were acknowledged by the 1980 revision of the 1973 Employment and Training Act. In 1973, the broad aim had been to assist young people leaving education to make 'a satisfactory transition from education to work'. The 1980 revision was more precise and related to the reality of that time:

- to seek to ensure that pupils, students and staff of schools and colleges are fully aware of the demands that working life is likely to make on young people entering employment and on the scope and range of opportunities available to them;
- to provide vocational guidance to pupils and students at appropriate stages during their educational life in association with schools and colleges;

- to help young people leaving schools and colleges and those who are unemployed to find employment, education or training or places on appropriate schemes.

The Society of Education Officers was among those to express disappointment with the new guidance. Its members would have liked to see an increase in the age range of the service to include all under 20 and the setting of a date by which all career officers must be trained and qualified.

Dealing with youth unemployment was to dominate the work of the Service during the 1980s. In March 1980, the number of unemployed school leavers in Great Britain was 290,300, about 12 per cent of girls and 5 per cent of boys. The 'bulge' in the birth rate meant that the number of school leavers would peak in 1981. Economists such as Santosh Mukhenjie, Leueslon and Stouer were forecasting that 2.5 million additional workers would seek to enter the labour market within the decade.

Discussion and argument about what was to be done was dramatically interrupted in 1981 when anxiety and frustration boiled over into riots in Brixton, London and Toxteth, Liverpool, shocking the nation. Careers officers may have been shocked but they were not surprised. Kevin Devine, the President of the Institute of Careers Officers, quoted from the Chief Constable of Liverpool's annual report, released shortly before the riots: 'I am confident that relationships with all sections of the community are in a very healthy position and I do not see any serious difficulties developing in the future' (Devine 1981). The youth unemployment crisis and the economic disparity it engendered had been conveniently ignored. Kevin Devine, however, described it as 'a prescription for further chaos and confusion, a social outrage which is to cause youngsters to be the victims of a society which appears to have no place for them'.

This reflected the views of careers officers in day-to-day contact with the 301,100 young people registered with them in September 1981. As the Department of Employment's Annual Report of 1980–81 pointed out, the Careers Service was experiencing profound change. As the number of school leavers reached a peak during this period, prospects for them worsened and the consequent increase in YOP places and other special measures put heavy pressure on the Service. Demand for traditional guidance work in schools also quickened.

For the first time since 1974, however, there was no increase in the staffing of the mainstream service. The number of strengthening posts (unemployment specialist careers officers) rose by a further 225 during the year, to reach a total of 1,065 professional and clerical posts. The total staff of the Service in 1981 was 5,080, of whom 2,640 were careers officers.

The effect of the increased workload was intriguing. Morale was high; productivity increased to meet demand. Despite the pressure, many developments took place; the computer system J11G/CAL was introduced, improved careers teacher training led to the introduction of a diploma in careers education; Coventry, for example, experimented with basing careers officers in schools and colleges.

At this time, the Department of Employment's Careers Service Branch was placing emphasis on improved management, the element said to be available from the Branch itself and its largely civil service trained inspectorate. Bert Johnson, the Head of Branch, opened the debate in the June edition of *In Service Training* (Johnson 1981). Pat White contributed her ILEA experience based on a version of 'Management by Objectives' (White 1981). Discussion widened to encompass the need for better co-ordination of MSC and DE activities and a stronger role for the Branch itself (Peck 1981).

Much of the background to this debate lay in the demands made by, and the increasing influence of, the MSC. The original chairman, Richard O'Brien, a moderate and concerned industrialist, was replaced by David Young, appointed by Mrs Thatcher. His rather more proactive, some might say aggressive, style matched that of the new Secretary of State, Norman Tebbit, who had replaced James Prior. Between 1974 and 1981, MSC's staff had increased from an original 19,000 to 24,250, a total of 26 per cent. Many in the Careers Service and in other local authority services, especially the Youth Service, resented this exponential growth, which had certainly not been matched in their own front-line bases.

Friction between local authority services and the MSC absorbed a disproportionate amount of the energy which should have been devoted to tackling unemployment in the early 1980s. Teachers wrote to newspapers complaining that they and their pupils were denied knowledge of opportunities until the last minute; youth workers felt doubts about what they believed was undue pressure on young people to accept places on schemes. There was a lack of co-ordination. The MSC saw itself as the co-ordinating element but this was simply not acceptable to education and local government in general. Some suggested a 'Youth Employment Council' (Peck 1981), with representatives of DE, DES and MSC charged with preventing overlap and promoting cohesion. A Department for Education and Employment might have been ideal.

The Careers Service, more directly involved than the Youth Service, fared better in many ways: mutual interdependence with MSC officials at local level ensured co-operation day to day on behalf of clients and providers but even here there were frequent misunderstandings. One concerned the Joblibraries, first mooted in 1979 as a way of providing careers information in Jobcentres on a self-service basis through the Careers and Occupational Information Centre from which Careers Services and schools were already supplied. The idea was sound, even laudable. The ICO offered co-operation on the understanding that the experiment should also involve local careers libraries (run by Careers Services) and the library service (already co-operating with the Careers Service).

As the experiment developed, however, it became apparent that these would be no joint projects. Tom Coates, Sheffield's Principal Careers Officer, wrote privately in June 1981 that although he was involved in talks to set up a joint venture in the careers office, MSC would eventually set up their own job library. They did. The development was eventually stopped after an investigation by Sir Derek Rayner's unit, set up by Mrs Thatcher to reduce waste and duplication. This was a small but not insignificant example of a fundamental weakness in government policy. Forced to pour money into combating unemployment, they chose to do so through their own agency, the MSC, but without relinquishing their original intention of reducing public expenditure on local authority services.

For its part, the MSC, often innovative and inventive (sometimes dubbed 'buccaneering'), grew impatient with local authorities, especially their departmental approach. They also realised that their local consultative arrangements, District Manpower Committees, were incapable of absorbing and reflecting local opinion and expertise.

The Commission had been aware for some time that its Youth Opportunities Programme, never designed for the numbers it carried in 1980, was quite inadequate. In May 1981, it issued *A New Training Initiative*, a consultative paper proposing three major objectives for the nation:

We must develop skill training in such a way as to enable young people entering at different stages and with different educational attainments to acquire agreed standards of skills appropriate to the jobs available and provide them with a basis for progression through further training.

We must move towards a position where all young people under the age of 18 have the opportunity of continuing in full-time education or entering a period of planned work experience, combined with related training and education.

We must open up widespread opportunities for adults, whether employed, unemployed or returning to work to acquire, update or increase their skills and knowledge during their working lives.

The consultation period which followed resulted in 1,000 written submissions. 'A New Training Initiative: An Agenda for Action' followed in December 1981 and included the basis of the Youth Training Scheme (YTS).

The Institute of Careers Officers welcomed the proposals, but was concerned about some of the 'social' measures contained in the detail. They opposed a proposal to prevent 16-year-old summer leavers from claiming benefit before September; the level of allowance (£750 per year, which was thought to be too low), the position of Easter leavers (felt to be put at a disadvantage), and the threat of benefit sanctions where only training places could be offered.

The next stage in the process was for the MSC to set up a 'Youth Task Group' on which the Careers Service was represented by Pat White, President of ICO and Principal Careers Officer for the Inner London Education Authority. The Youth Task Group reported in April 1982. Its report described the new scheme, drew lessons from its predecessors and authorised new national and local machinery within which the newly merged divisions of the Commission should consult and co-ordinate the work of the local committees. The Careers Service was to be represented on the national and local boards, which were to be established on 1 September 1982.

Throughout 1982 and 1983, the introduction of YTS dominated the Careers Service. Fortunately, the 'bulge' in school leaver number had passed its peak. Vocational guidance interview numbers fell only a little, however, as awareness of the need for careful career planning spread throughout schools and colleges. Greater awareness of the importance of the Service as an agent of government policy probably accounted for much of the further increase in staffing which took place. By the end of 1983, the regular establishment had risen from 5,310 to 5,440 and continued to be strengthened by an additional 1,060 posts directly funded by the Department of Employment. The Careers Service was larger and perhaps more influential than ever before.

That influence increased further as a result of the appointment of a new minister, Peter Morrison. Initially there was a good deal of concern in the ICO and amongst principal careers officers generally about the appointment. Morrison was a parliamentary under secretary, rather than a minister of state, suggesting a demotion for Careers Service affairs and he gained an early reputation as a right-wing critic of the Service who intended to change attitudes and bang heads together where necessary. This initial impression seemed to be confirmed when his speech to the 1983 ICO Conference began with a list of criticisms from employers, followed by a reference to careers officers being regarded by many as 'social engineers'. He went on, however, to declare his intention to improve the reputation of the Service amongst employers, local authorities and young people.

His most successful and practical suggestion for doing so concerned local authorities. To encourage elected members to take a closer interest, he announced his intention to meet the chair of the education committee of every Service inspected in the future and his target of making personal contact with one in three chairs within one year. This represented a considerable personal workload, but proved to be excellent value. The process of briefing chairs, undertaken by principal careers officers and chief education officers, did much to inform local councillors. The meetings, held in Morrison's private office, were well-conducted and many chairs left there more inclined to want a Careers Service of which they could be proud. Morrison's goal of producing 'a more cost-effective, efficient and responsive Service accorded proper status within individual authorities' was gradually being reached.

He also defused anxiety about the Rayner Report (Sir Derek Rayner's efficiency unit had reviewed the 'overlap' between the MSC and the Careers Service and recommended a review). Morrison announced that he would wait until the YTS had become well-established and then consider the success of the 'Christmas Undertaking' before deciding about the need for and terms of any review.

Morrison was as good as his word. He developed a genuine interest in the Careers Service, made good working and personal relationships with many representative principal careers officers, especially Derek Mills, a member of the MSC Special Programmes Board, and Tom Coates, the Institute's President. He held many informal meetings in order to gain impressions of coal-face opinion and strengthened and improved the morale of the Careers Service Branch. In a letter to principal careers officers dated February 1985 he wrote: 'As the minister responsible for Careers Service matters, I am writing to you personally to express my thanks, and those of the Secretary of State and the Chairman of the MSC, to you and your staff for all the work you have done for young people over the past twelve months. In particular, I am grateful for the work your Service has done with the Youth Training Scheme. The Scheme itself is a splendid success and the Careers Service certainly can and should take their share of the credit.'

The momentum provided by responding to change, and the stimulus of being in the spotlight, spilled over into the wider aspects of careers education and guidance. The regional teams created to provide in-service training for teachers, led by HMI and Careers Service inspectors, evolved into joint in-service training committees of LEAs throughout the regions. Many (the West Midlands was a good example) began concentrating on short residential courses for headteacher and deputies. This did much to strengthen careers education in the curriculum and improve the effectiveness of careers officers and the teachers involved. In 1983, the National Union of Teachers devoted the whole of its annual *Career Guide* to the New Training Initiative, and the implications of the employment situation for teachers preparing young people for an uncertain future.

Careers information improved, largely through co-operation between the Careers and Occupational Information Centre and local Careers Services. Bulk purchase arrangements and more readily available material held in and distributed from careers offices did much to improve careers libraries in schools. The size of the Careers Service also increased to an overall cadre of 6,200, of whom about 3,600 were qualified careers officers. This made it the only sector of local government to actually increase in size and resources during this period.

All this momentum and expansion of the careers field contributed to an even wider debate on education for work at local and national level. The impetus had come from the Government with David Young, Chairman of the MSC, keen to see vocational preparation in schools, and from Geoffrey Holland, who remained a powerhouse of ideas and solutions to problems. The Department of Employment played a part under strong leadership from a new Permanent Secretary, Michael Quinlan, transferred from the Ministry of Defence and ready to operate the Department under a 'command structure'. But David Young's approach was challenged by, among others, Clare Short, an ex-civil servant, then Director of the charity 'Youthaid'. She warned that schools which became too responsive to employers' needs would be adopting an approach tantamount to: 'Tell us what you want and we will do it to them.' Some teachers and many youth workers, whose place in YTS had been acknowledged by the DES Circular of 1982, tended to share this sceptical view.

Tony Watts, the Director of NICEC, took a more measured approach. In *Education, Unemployment and the Future of Work* (Watts 1984), he pointed out the paradox that unemployment had strengthened rather than weakened the bonds between education and work. He examined four models for the future: the unemployment scenario, the leisure scenario, the work scenario and the employment scenario. His general conclusion was that, whatever their future, young people should begin discussing it well before they leave school, and that the way society makes its living could be a useful study in itself.

At a more practical level he contributed *Work Experience in Schools* (Watts 1984), warning that clear policies were required if places required for YTS were not to be lost to pupils seeking valuable experience during their school career. Using quotations perceptively: 'work experience is a novelty, employment is a habit', and 'the new romance of work: work will stimulate curiosity and promote learning, whereas school stultifies them', he helped ensure that schools were able to contribute and respond to the wider debate on the evolution of work and employment.

Donald Super brought the American perspective to bear with *Self-realisation through Work and Leisure Roles* (Super 1985), pointing out that work might be so organised that workers might be honoured for their work, but many at all levels would gladly devote themselves to other roles as 'homeworkers and leisurites'. His argument for greater discussion and planning was summed up in the quotation 'If you don't know where you're going, you'll end up somewhere else.'

Kenneth Roberts' contribution was typically down-to-earth. In *School Leavers and Their Prospects* (Roberts 1985), he rejected leisure solutions as unnecessary and unworkable: jobs, training and education were what was required. He argued that aspirations had been unblocked by education at a time when the consolation for educational failure – entry into well paid, if monotonous, jobs – had been withdrawn. He also questioned the view that young people would be better placed if schools went back to basics; if all were better accomplished in reading, writing and arithmetic, and disciplined into habitual obedience. With his usual sharp historical perspective, he pointed out that: 'Elementary schooling did not save the school leavers of the 1930s from unemployment.'

But the economic argument was persuasive, especially to politicians. It was encapsulated by a seminal paper published in 1984 over the joint signatures of Geoffrey Holland (MSC) and John Cassells of the National Economic Development Office. *Competence and Competition* (Institute of Manpower Studies 1984), written by Chris Hayes, Alan Anderson and Nicky Founder, compared the successful training systems of Japan, the United States and Germany with that of the UK. The underlying theme was that technology is increasingly transferable from one country to another and competition is increasingly between workforces. What had seemed, therefore, to be a purely economic debate, was essentially about education. At a time when many would argue, as Enoch Powell did, about 'the heresy that education is useful and the corollary that education produces economic wellbeing', this was remarkable. It was also prophetic; the language used and the recommendations made would have been familiar to the new Blair government in 1997.

Competence and Competition did not mention the Careers Service, but drew an inevitable response from careers officers who had, for some time, been discussing education in these terms. They commented upon the need for a department of education and training, the weakness of the 'Training and Information Framework' which processed local statistics, and the inadequacy of the MSC's Area Manpower Boards. They also expressed their concern that, once more, decisions were about to be taken on their area of expertise without consultation. For example, Lord Young's Committee on the 14–18 age group was meeting at the time but contained no one from the Careers Service and did not take evidence.

The situation was well summarised by Stewart Ranson, whose team at the Institute of Local Government Studies at the University of Birmingham had been researching planning for the 16–19 age group:

> Structured change in the economy and the enduring collapse of the youth labour market have transformed the routine transition of young people to work. The education of this transition age group has now moved to the centre of policy-making in central and local government.

He went on to admire 'the vitality and imagination with which the Service is responding to, as well as shaping, a period of change' (Ranson and Ribbins 1985).

Within the Service there was some feeling of frustration that this vitality and imagination was insufficiently recognised when policy was being forged, and that the structural position of the Service – confined to one of 30 Branches in the Department of Employment – constrained its influence and artificially restricted its growth. Resentment centred on Careers Service Branch. Relations with the Branch had deteriorated since the late 1970s and had at times become openly hostile. For example, Birmingham went so far as to refuse to be inspected on the grounds that the Inspectorate had nothing to contribute to the management or improvement of its Service.

The Branch recognised the difficulty and issued a paper explaining its position for discussion at the Middlesbrough conference of the Institute of Careers Officers. But, while the paper bravely invited discussion on how the Branch was viewed and whether there were things it was not doing, it described a limited brief and placed what was thought to be an undue emphasis on performance indicators, the Memorandum of Guidance and a plea for understanding of its limited role with ministers.

The new Head of Careers Service Branch reinforced the impression when he was appointed in April 1986. His introductory statement emphasised 'Inspection and the promotion of efficiency' and the need to be 'cost effective'. His objectives were:

- To see that Careers Service vocational guidance work is practical, realistic and effective.
- To secure effective work with employers and placing work generally.
- To see that the Careers Service plays a full and effective part in the successful delivery of YTS.
- To secure effective management practices in the Careers Service.

No one objected to this, particularly as he went on to talk about working more closely with the Department of Education and Science (DES). It just seemed so inappropriate and unimaginative. While the Institute of Local Government Studies and the Local Government Training Board were proposing the transfer of the Service to the DES, the Unit for the Development of Adult Continuing Education was pointing out that every time a student fails to receive appropriate guidance and enrols on an inappropriate course, teaching resources and the student's time are wasted. The Careers Service Branch was restricting itself to a wholly administrative role and taking no part in the wider debate.

There was, of course, little likelihood of the DES assuming control. Ever since 1973, that Department had assiduously observed the civil service convention of avoiding stepping on the toes of another Department. The Department of Employment's policy of containment, cloaked by a desire only to safeguard their minister's statutory duty, ignored what Ranson and Ribbins called 'this quite unique social function' (1985) and its potential. Indeed, the Branch had by 1986 withdrawn their Regional Representatives and reduced their staff by half.

Perhaps it was the contrast between the Department of Employment and the Manpower Services Commission which lay at the heart of the frustration felt in the Careers Service. The 1984 White Paper 'Training for Jobs' had described a cohesive pattern emerging from the Technical and Vocational Education Initiative and the Certificate of Pre-vocational Education. MSC control over work-related further education was increasing. The Careers and Occupational Information Centre expanded its work in schools with the implication that information rather than guidance was the way forward (Peck 1984). There was continuing suspicion that the MSC would, when convenient, take over the Careers Service using the 3,000 or so trained and qualified careers officers to fuel its own further expansion, while removing the sometimes critical interventions of principal careers officers to the otherwise rather bland meetings of the Area Manpower and Special Programmes Boards. This perceived threat bedevilled relationships. The threat was probably real enough. Daniel Lawrence, writing in *Local Government Studies* in 1993, believed that ministers considered a transfer of responsibility in 1986, but withdrew due to the likely strength of opposition.

A particular area of controversy between the Department of Employment, the MSC and the Careers Service was the question of who should provide educational and vocational advice for adults. The 1973 Act allowed careers services to offer a service to adults providing they had the means to do so and some did, even as early as 1974. In 1979, for example, it was estimated that 135,000 adults approached a careers officer for help: 42,000 received formal guidance interviews and 93,000 received information. The MSC's Occupational Guidance Units carried out 54,101 first interviews and 4,402 subsequent interviews during the same period. These numbers increased, with Careers Services such as Birmingham, Sheffield and Harrow leading the way. Occupational Guidance Units were disbanded in 1981. Educational guidance services emerged, funded from a variety of sources such as the European Social Fund, the Urban Aid Programme and imaginative use of Department of Education and Science funding by local education authorities. This was known generally as 'funny money' although, as Jonathon Brown, who became chairman of the Natioanl Association of Educational Guidance Services for Adults (NAEGA), pointed out, 'funny money isn't funny when it stops'.

NAEGA was formed in 1982 at the Association for Recurrent Education conference at Bretton Hall with support from a variety of interests, including the Open University, the library service and many Careers Services. The first president was Dorothy Eagleson of Northern Ireland. Jonathon Brown of Newcastle was the first chairman.

The 1985 report of the Unit for the Development of Adult and Continuing Education (UDACE) 'Helping Adults to Learn' helped focus the debate and involved the DES directly, while the coincidental issuing of the MSC's 'Adult Training Strategy' raised the spectre of confusing and overlapping services for adults. The UDACE report also described the Careers Service as having trained officers with expertise and access to information on entry requirements and opportunities.

A subsequent report, based on 220 responses to the original document, and called 'The Challenge of Change', proposed the establishment of local networks. It seemed to many that, to avoid duplication and facilitate co-operation, principal careers officers should be responsible and accountable for running the proposed networks. The Institute of Careers Guidance and many local consortia increased their effort to train adult careers advisers. Consequently, activity increased. The MSC, already enquiring into the provision of information, advice and guidance for 18–24-year-olds, took an interest, with David Tinsley, the new Deputy Director (originally recruited from Birmingham LEA), playing an important part, but the Employment Department, whose official line was always that the Careers Service should concentrate on those under 18, took no part in the public debate. The strength of belief in the need to provide an all-age service was one of several themes noted by Ranson and Ribbins.

Ranson and Ribbins also challenged the perceived ambitions of the MSC in other important areas. In *Servicing Careers in a Post-employment Society* (1985) they examined ten local Careers Services, interviewing careers officers, teachers, education officers and MSC officials in their investigation of structure and organisation. Their conclusion was that the Service performed a 'unique social function' and that careers officers operated as 'strategic change agents'. They argued that the 'plurality of roles' was important in fulfilling the primary function of mediating between the individual and the socio-economic system. They concluded also that the work of the Service remained essentially educational, that it should be located in local government and in the education department, but with a wider role as part of a central planning team located in the Chief Executive's, Planning or Economic Development Department.

Ranson and Ribbins drew attention to an area of practice which was to surface again ten years later in the minds of those who originated the Connexions strategy. They found a strong belief amongst unemployment specialist careers officers in the importance of advocacy on behalf of young people. Many were convinced of their need to tackle problems in the home and personal lives of their clients before career choice and job-finding could be addressed. In some cases, this involved referring them to other agencies.

Their final remarks were that:

> By clarifying and developing its function, roles and organisation, the Careers Service can regard the future positively, contributing as it will, strategically, to the reforming of education, training and employment in the interests of young people and adults experiencing a period of structural change in society.
>
> (Ranson and Ribbins 1985: 232)

In July 1986, the Secretary of State issued a draft revision of the Memorandum of Guidance to local authorities under the 1973 Act. Most respondents, the Association of County Councils, the Association of Municipal Authorities and the Institute of Careers Officers, were critical of the quality of the draft. When the final version appeared in 1988, it was virtually the same as the previous revision in 1980.

The Institute of Careers Officers was keen to improve the performance of the Service overall, and produced a proposed Code of Practice in 1987 as a result of discussions held at the 1986 Conference. Set out in terms of principles, practice and implementation, this paper covered the rights of clients and the responsibility of the adviser for ethical and efficient practice. It proposed a complaints procedure, which was to include the power of expulsion from the Institute (ICO 1987). The Code was debated thoroughly at Branch level over the two-year period 1986–1988, aided by contributions from Terry Collins, who described his vision of a college-based 'Education Counsellor' working in an all-age Careers Service, firmly based in education (Collins 1986), and by Colin Taylor of the Scottish Branch, who argued strongly for the retention of placing in jobs and analysed the positions of 'realist' and 'non directive' practitioners against current theories of career choice (Taylor 1988). Both emphasised the need for more discussion of ideas and debate about the professional ethos. The revised Code of Practice was finally adopted at the 1988 Annual Conference.

Central to the Code of Practice was 'equal opportunities'. Not new, of course; the concern of careers advisers for minorities – disabled people, ethnic minorities and those with economic and social disadvantages – had always underpinned their work. But in the mid-1980s, equal opportunities had attracted a far wider following, especially in large urban centres such as Birmingham.

Birmingham, the base of the President, Peter Jones, provided the venue for the 1987 ICO Conference, with the theme 'Facing the Future'. Equal opportunities for all, especially ethnic minorities and disadvantaged adults, dominated discussion (Surridge 1987). There was also a strong municipal influence, with the local government spokesman reminding careers officers that 'Careers stood at the heart of the education service', and making a strong plea for services to do more to provide for the needs of adults. The Conference closed with an address by John Banham, Director General of the CBI, describing his personal view of how Great Britain could find its place in the technological revolution. A personal view, but indicative of the forthcoming CBI report 'Towards a Skills Revolution', which was to help bring careers education and guidance well to the fore and influence government thinking on the future of the Careers Service.

Other exciting developments were taking place. The 1987 White Papers 'Working Together – Education and Training' and 'Working Together for a Better Future', issued jointly by the Education and Employment Departments, led to every LEA having a written policy on careers education and guidance by the end of 1988. The practice of both departments working together in this one area of endeavour was by no means the rule. Initiatives came thick and fast but co-ordination was lacking. There were rumours of 'private industry councils' in the offing based on an American model. The Manpower Services Commission came to an end in 1988 and its Director, Geoffrey Holland, became Permanent Secretary to the Department of Employment.

One import from the US arrived in March of that year when the government introduced its version of the 'Boston Compact' designed to bring schools and employers closer under the 'Action in Cities' programme and to improve pupil motivation by pointing their ambitions towards potential employers. Kay Stratton, who had managed the scheme in Boston and was commissioned to introduce it to Britain, was originally surprised to learn about the Careers Service (her achievement in Boston had been based on training teachers to become careers advisers where there was no Careers Service), but involved Careers Services in most of the twelve pilots which were established over four years.

The CBI vocational education task force produced an interim report on the lines previously signalled to the ICO by John Banham, which was to lead to

'Towards a Skills Revolution'. This report was to influence the pattern of training, introduce the concept of 'Careership' and ultimately highlight and affect fundamentally the pattern of careers education and guidance. The American pattern of 'Private Industry Councils' was hurriedly adapted to manifest itself in the United Kingdom as 'Training and Enterprise Councils' (Local Enterprise Councils in Scotland).

It is worth pausing to take stock of the position in 1989. Terry Collins, the Institute's President in that year, marked it as a turning point thus: 'When books about social history come to be written, there is always an attempt to identify when a different age dawned . . . 1988–89 must be one of those years' (Collins 1989). Collins picked out a number of changes relevant to the world of careers education and guidance, which he regarded as part of a better future emerging from the 1980s. He included in this the arrival of the 'post-industrial age', a national curriculum in schools, a national foundation of education and business partnerships, associations of guidance practitioners sitting down together (Terry Collins was instrumental in setting up the Standing Conference of Associations of Guidance in Educational Settings), and the arrival of Training and Enterprise Councils (TECs).

TECs were a manifestation of what was happening generally in the United Kingdom at that time. The Conservative government was at its strongest. Sceptical about local government and local politicians in particular, it believed in the ability of business representatives to provide leadership and initiative in local affairs. Opposition was discouraged. The idea was borrowed from the Private Industry Councils in use in the United States but the theory behind them seemed to stem from a distortion of Adam Smith's belief that good would flow automatically from the efforts of groups of successful entrepreneurs working on behalf of a community or communities. Elitism was explicit. Members of the TECs were to be appointed and would come from a single occupational and social group. They were to be of 'Managing Director' level. No personnel directors need apply.

Local authorities were to be represented by their chief executives – local politicians were not encouraged – nor were chief education officers. While LEAs gave generous support in helping TECs get underway, there was unease throughout the education world. This was justified: provoked by what John McLeod of the Association of Metropolitan Authorities described as 'media hype excessive even for the Department of Employment' (McLeod 1989), and a persisting feeling of exclusion.

Local Careers Services were totally excluded. Nothing even approaching the right of attendance of principal careers officers at meetings of MSC Area Manpower Boards was envisaged. Heads of Careers Services were simply summoned to Moorfoot to be informed, eventually, and to be asked to co-operate. They did so, because when the TEC Chairmen were appointed and needed to know about education and the way it related to industry and commerce, it was to the Careers Service that many of them turned.

TECs were to be important to the Careers Service: no one could be sure how important. But planning to deal with the relative shortage of young people (due to worsen until at least 1993) would clearly require careful local co-operation. TECs were to be involved in career guidance: no one knew just how much involved. Some, including the majority of the CBI Task Force, felt they should take over the Careers Service entirely.

As the new decade began, therefore, the focus of the Careers Service was on the employment prospects for a declining number of school leavers and their need for careful careers guidance on the one hand and, on the other hand, administrative arrangements which could ensure better planning and co-operation at national and local level.

At national level, there was concern about relations between the Department of Employment and the Department of Education and Science. Norman Fowler's resignation from the DE led to the appointment of Michael Howard. Fowler and McGregor (at DES) had been working closely together on ideas (such as training credits) to supersede the Youth Training Scheme. But it was not known how well the two departments would work together with Employment under new leadership. The effects of policy differences were most likely to be felt at local level where the relationship between LEAs and the new TECs seemed likely to be problematic.

In her message to members of the Institute of Careers Officers at the beginning of 1990, the President, Avril Rimmer, stressed the need for every young person between 16 and 18 to be either in full-time education or a job with training. She listed the topics on which the ICO should attempt to influence policy as: 'Training and Enterprise Councils; the National Curriculum and Careers Education within it; the development of a Single European Market; Personal Action Plans; Records of Achievement and Summaries of Guidance; NVQs, Youth Training and Development in the field of adult guidance and training' (Rimmer 1989). She closed with a reference to the needs of young people and adults and their requirement for strong independent career advice, already acknowledged by the CBI Vocational and Training Task Force. As usual, the Careers Service was involved in the national debate on education and employment and expected to be involved in changes to policy and practice. There was nothing to suggest, however, that the Service itself would undergo fundamental change as part of this process.

The announcement of a review of the Careers Service was made by Tim Eggar, the Minister of State for Employment, on 10 May 1990. He announced an internal review to be carried out by civil servants who were to report in

September 1990. Many within the Service felt that the growing importance of career advice merited a review of the arrangement for providing this function as a whole. There was disquiet, however, about the internal nature of the review and the restriction in scope to the Careers Service alone.

It was felt that Sir Brian Nicholson of the CBI (and previously Chairman of the Manpower Services Commission) had been influential in provoking the review. Sir Geoffrey Holland, the DE Permanent Secretary, later referred to its origin at a seminar at 10 Downing Street at which careers guidance was discussed in the context of anticipated demographic, commercial and technological change in the 1990s (Nicholson probably took part). Holland went on to say that, while the Careers Service in the UK was already among the best, it should adopt some features provided in other countries if it was to remain so. He stressed that the outcome of the review was in no way predetermined, nor was it linked to any strategy concerning the future of local government in general.

Local government was to feature strongly in the discussion from the outset. The overwhelming view in the Careers Service was that it should continue to be based in education, although there was unease about the Conservative government's attitude to LEAs, reportedly seen as dispensable by some ministers. Some heads of Careers Services also felt themselves constrained by LEA structures, designed as they were largely for management of schools.

When Daniel Lawrence of Nottingham University came to analyse the whole process in 1993, he did so under the title *The Rise and Fall of the Local Government Careers Service* (Lawrence 1993), pointing out that it had taken 64 years for the Careers Service to become a wholly local government responsibility in 1974.

That there was dissatisfaction with the LEA stewardship amongst civil servants seems undeniable. Valerie Bayliss, Professor Associate in the Department of Education Studies at the University of Sheffield, and previously the civil servant largely instrumental in bringing about the changes, said as much when she delivered the Centre for Guidance Studies' Annual Lecture on 16 December 1999. Describing the removal of LEA control in 1994, Bayliss referred to

> a control which I am bound to say too often confined the [LEA Careers Services] to a quiet backwater. This was the service that, before 1994, displayed many large variations in the level of resources devoted to it and even larger variations in the quality of service to clients. Moreover, there was no observable relationship between the level of spend and quality of delivery.
>
> (Bayliss 1999: 1)

Whatever the feelings of ministers and civil servants at that time, the internal review was set up swiftly after the minister's announcement. The civil servant appointed to lead was Don Bruce, Deputy Regional Director of the Department of Employment in its Yorkshire and Humberside region.

What he thought and what he eventually recommended remains a matter of conjecture. His report was never made public. There was persistent rumour and gossip during 1990, however, that Bruce favoured the 'radical alternative' (radical, that is, in the light of current developments elsewhere) of retaining the status quo: leaving the Service within LEA control.

Meanwhile, many within the Service were developing ideas for the future. Colin Thompson, the County Careers Officer for Surrey, commissioned Cooper and Lybrand to study the position in his own and two other authorities. They recommended that Careers Services should become limited companies with an 'arm's length' relationship to local authorities, part owned by LEAs and TECs. The United Kingdom Heads of Careers Services Association and the renamed Institute of Careers Guidance began to review alternatives and consider attitudes to TECs and their involvement.

The main speaker at the Institute's conference in September 1989 was Tony Blair, Secretary of State for Employment and Member of Parliament for the constituency in which the President, Avril Rimmer, lived and worked. He spoke of his own and his leader, Neil Kinnock's, enthusiasm for education and training. On the subject of the future of the Careers Service he was non-committal.

When the consultative process on the future of the Service was announced in March 1991, it proposed only three alternative models for consideration: control by TECs, privatisation or ownership by TEC/LEA partnerships. Daniel Lawrence (Lawrence 1993) has pointed out that, despite the history of the 64 years leading to local government control of the Service and their relatively successful 17 years of management since 1974, the option of local government control was not on the agenda. Most observers were unconvinced by the Secretary of State's (Michael Howard) claim that 'the introduction of market principles is needed to sharpen managerial practice which, in some areas, is below an acceptable standard' was the reason for change. It seemed part of the process which had started with the TVEI in the mid-1980s, of moving much control and influence over education from local to central government, and from teachers to employers. Lawrence (1993) has suggested that it was also judged politically necessary, in the wake of the poll tax, to reduce local tax levels. Lawrence also believed that, as part of this trend, ministers originally wished to transfer Careers Services directly to TECs, who resisted this on the grounds that they had quite enough to do in establishing their own viability at that time.

When the White Paper 'Education and Training in the Twenty-first Century' was published in May 1991, it announced that the government would introduce legislation to remove responsibility to run Careers Services from LEAs, and make the Secretary of State for Employment responsible for providing the service in a variety of ways. In April 1992, the Department of Employment announced informally the government's intention to implement the White Paper's recommendation. In May, the Queen's Speech at the opening of Parliament included the Trade Union Reform and Employment Rights Bill (which was to contain a clause on the future of the Careers Service) in the government's programme.

In many ways, 1991/92 was an unhappy year for the Careers Service and those within and around it. Many careers officers, aware of the value of their work and feeling themselves productive and well-managed within the resources available to them, were dismayed by the government's decision and the criticism of their values and competence which it implied. They could find no consolation in knowing that colleges of further education and other parts of the education service were also in turmoil.

TECs were proving difficult to work with; staffed by a mixture including disillusioned seconded civil servants and a variety of individuals who had successfully sought a change from commerce and industry, they were united only in stressing their enterprising outlook and freedom from accountability in the usual public service sense. Many members of the seconded staff felt insecure and were managing a painful transition to a quasi-private sector philosophy. A TEC National Council had emerged, however, and was capable of contributing to policy on Careers Service matters.

Heads of Careers Services were well placed to play their part through the United Kingdom Heads of Careers Services Association. The Association had originated from a statement of common purpose prepared by the West Midlands regional group of principal careers officers and consisted of regional representatives who met throughout the year and held an annual conference. They had established their credentials by producing, with the support of the local authority associations, an annual analysis of the destinations of all school leavers.

Roger Little, the Chair of the Association, Paul Chubb, President of the Institute of Careers Guidance, and Graham Hayle, representing the TEC National Council, came together to produce a joint policy paper in 1992. This paper, *Delivering Quality Careers Guidance* (ICG *et al*. 1992), set out what should be expected of a Careers Service in the circumstances likely to emerge from the legislative process. It provided a basis on which the LEA/TEC partnership could be built and covered:

- What young people have the right to expect

- Primary responsibility for aspects of careers education and guidance.
- Performance measures.
- Client satisfaction.
- Services for adults.
- Services for other clients (schools, colleges, employers, etc.).

The difficult process of accommodation had begun.

The participants had little option. What was so apparent in the Summer of 1992 was the power of the Department of Employment, whose ministers and officials were determined to have their way. In the light of this, ministers were able to appear relaxed and reasonable. Gillian Shephard, the Secretary of State for Employment, invited officers of ICG and UK HoCSA to meet her informally in July. Patrick McLoughlin, her junior minister responsible for the Careers Service, offered to write an article for *Careers Officer* aimed at mitigating the anxiety of careers officers. Alan Davies, the head of Careers Service Branch, was proving himself an honest and capable negotiator who had the confidence of his supervisors.

The way to success for those attempting to modify the Government's proposals was likely to be by assiduous negotiation and attention to detail. Meetings with a group of opposition MPs confirmed this position. Frank Dobson, who led this group, made it clear that the government's majority meant that amendments, even at the committee stage, would be difficult and would require careful tactics if the opposition was to avoid being outvoted.

Civil servants were clearly disappointed that they were unable to get the Bill into the current Parliamentary session but they announced that it would be published in October. When it was published, it was described by David Whitbread, the remarkably able Education Officer of the Association of County Councils, as 'Henry VIII Legislation'. It would enable the Secretary of State to do exactly what she wanted. This wise warning was issued to ICG and UK HoCSA at a briefing meeting with the Local Authority Associations in the Autumn of 1992.

While the Careers Service continued with its pragmatic approach, it did so against a background which was almost surreal. Faced with the realisation that the Service must receive 'the cure for which there is no known illness', representatives of Heads of Service and the ICG had to listen to vague ministerial allusions to a flawed Careers Service requiring legislation to address its weaknesses. Why else would the government wish to reform it?

Against this background, the Trade Union and Employment Rights Bill received a first reading (a formality only) in November 1992 and a second reading on 17 November. ICG opened its campaign by appointing an 'Employment Bill Task Force' to co-ordinate activity and make rapid decisions when necessary. With an important decision of principle, it was decided to pay the employers of Paul Chubb and Rob Stokes for some of the time they would henceforth spend on lobbying. Perhaps this marked an acceptance of the fact that the honorary officers alone could not carry on the traditions of the Institute. The appointment of Cathi Bereznicki as chief executive in August 1993 had been the first important step in this direction.

The UK Heads of Service Group acted similarly, setting up its 'Bill Group' to draft amendments under the chairmanship of Roger Little of Herefordshire and Worcestershire. The chair and vice chair were to co-ordinate lobbying and frequent and regular briefing of members.

And so the Bill began its progress through the committee stage, with lobbyists armed with a variety of careful amendments covering questions such as: access to educational institutions; fit and proper persons to be appointed to give careers advice; summaries of guidance; details of charging for services and ways of deterring predatory bidders. A copy of a policy document 'The New Careers Service', and a sheet of detailed proposed amendments, were sent to every member of the Standing Committee. The process was made difficult for the lobbyists by the realisation that every proposed improvement to the legislation was regarded as opposition by the government.

Sam Galbraith, Angela Eagle and David Hanson, all members of Labour's Employment Committee, proposed the amendments but withdrew them in the face of implacable opposition from Patrick McLoughlin, the Minister for State, working to a written brief. The Under Secretary of State, Michael Forsyth, and Derek Conway, also a member of the Whip's Office, conducted unrelated business throughout the debate, demonstrating their indifference and their complete confidence in their absolute majority.

What was actually being acted out was one small part of a much wider policy towards the public services in general. Ministers were interested only in seeing their policy enacted. Civil servants, faced with providing continuity of service within a workable framework, needed wide-ranging enabling legislation; they wished, therefore, to focus debate on the forthcoming Memorandum of Guidance rather than legislation itself. The House of Lords would provide the only possible forum for debate at the legislative stage.

The Committee Stage in the House of Lords was reached on 30 March, when the Bill was read. Baroness David and Lady Fisher led for the opposition. NALGO and the Local Authority Associations had joined ICG and the Heads of Service Group in preparing careful amendments. A number of careers officers were able to attend.

Debate centred first on the need for well-qualified careers officers trained specifically for their work. Baroness Seer, a veteran of the 1973 Bill, reminded the government of the Department of Employment's failure to train its own careers staff at that time. The quality of debate was high, but the lack of any prospect of achieving substantial change in the legislation soon became apparent. Apart from minor amendments on the right of access of disabled young people to careers officers, and administrative items such as the two-year period in which LEAs could continue to be responsible for Careers Services in cases where the new arrangements might break down, there were no amendments. In the closing debate, Lord Wedderburn observed that he had witnessed a most authoritarian stance being taken by the government and that they did not seem to realise just how authoritarian they had been. That summed it up.

After the frustration of all the efforts to amend the Bill in the House of Lords, it came as almost a relief to turn to the implementation of the Act, expected to receive Royal Assent in July 1993.

The campaign had been valuable, not least for the way it focused minds on what kind of Careers Service was needed. Opposition had been almost universal within the educational and guidance communities. Teachers, represented by NACGT, the teacher unions and individuals, had contributed a great deal. Tony Watts of NICEC and his colleagues had been influential, largely due to their fear of professional erosion and the potential breakdown of the valuable relationship between teachers and careers advisers. It seemed, at the time, that little progress had been made, but Valerie Bayliss, speaking at the University of Derby in November 2000, said emphatically that much modification had been achieved behind the scenes.

With hindsight it is possible to speculate on whether more change still might have been effected if careers advisers had placed more emphasis on the value of their job-knowledge, links with industry, and influence on benefit payments rather than the process of careers choice.

The Institute of Careers Guidance and the UK Heads of Careers Services had worked closely together throughout the process. Their approaches naturally differed to some extent but there was one topic on which they took quite different views. This was the question of a national council, seen by the Institute as a potentially powerful addition to the legislation and a safeguard for clients. The Post Office Users National Council was cited as an example of what might be achieved. Others shared this interest in a national council for careers education and counselling, notably the Royal Society of Arts (RSA). Christopher Ball, representing RSA, Tony Watts of NICEC and Paul Chubb, President of ICG were able to meet Gillian Shephard, the Secretary of State for Employment, to make their case.

The Heads of Service Association felt that the question of a national council was a distraction from the main business of the Bill. It seemed to them unlikely that such a body could ever have statutory powers or any other status within the legislation. They were quite happy to offer support to the RSA and ICG in their efforts to establish what eventually became the National Council for Careers Education and Counselling (generally known as the Guidance Council) but not to advocate its inclusion in statutory provision of the Careers Service.

Implementation had been in the minds of the Department of Employment's Careers Service Branch since the early stages of the legislative process. Alan Davies, the Head of Branch, had deployed his team carefully. Peter Heavyside, the chief inspector, had been working full-time on the Bill itself. John Harradance had produced 'What we are buying', a guide to the arrangements expected to apply. Stephen Holt was deputed to work out the detail of the contract, consulting with the heads of Careers Service and others as he did so.

The Careers Service Consultative Group, a body which contained representatives of Training Enterprise Councils, Local Authority Associations and Heads of Careers Service from Scotland, Wales and each English region, proved a useful conduit at this stage. There was much talk of 'Total Quality management', process, input, delivery and monitoring. The Department seemed anxious to avoid the problems it had experienced over the financial control and accountability of training enterprise councils.

The UK Heads of Careers Service Association had a clear vision of the shape of the new companies. In their policy paper 'The New Careers Service', they laid stress on the need for accountability, stability, impartiality and acceptability. This would require a structure which provided for locally representative boards, an identified head of service, careers advisers trained to national standards and government contracts to cover a reasonable length of time (three years was the period they had in mind: TECs had been hampered by one-year contracts, too short to allow proper planning).

While the efforts of the Careers Service were directed towards the practical problems of refining the legislation and then to facilitating its implementation, the wider debate about career guidance continued, but with a more political flavour than ever before. Conferences on provision for adult guidance, for example, were bedevilled by talk of 'markets in guidance' and 'guidance as market maker'. Junior ministers would describe careers advisers as similar to financial advisers (perhaps the only experience of personal counselling they themselves valued), and talked of the need to create a market by advertising and competition before adults would present themselves for advice. To careers advisers with full appointment books, forced by limited resources to make their adult clients wait for weeks before they could be interviewed, this was deeply frustrating. To them, the solution seemed simple. Rather than channel resources into a variety of organisations resting on precarious foundations built on 'funny money' (short-term hypothecated funding by TECs), demand should be met by funding Careers Services directly.

Two important pieces of academic work helped to clarify this debate and make a contribution to policy-making in the guidance field. Both stemmed from NICEC. Perhaps the most influential of these was a joint venture between NICEC and the Policy Studies Institute commissioned by the Department of Employment's Careers Service Branch and published in 1992. *The Economic Benefits of Careers Guidance* (NICEC 1992) examined four questions:

- What is guidance?
- What economic benefits might guidance yield?
- What evidence is there that it does so?
- What further research is needed?

Using research from the USA and British research from between the wars, this paper set out clearly the benefits to individuals, to education and training providers, to employers, and to governments. It provided a basis on which policy-makers, administrators, politicians and practitioners could conduct discussions at national and local level, and on which decision-making could be based. John Killeen of NICEC played a major part in this initiative. Tony Watts was closely involved and helped ensure its wider dissemination.

Tony Watts wrote the other seminal paper 'The Impact of the New Right: Policy Challenges Confronting Careers Guidance in England and Wales', which was published in September 1991 (Watts 1991). Commentaries subsequently appeared in *The Careers Officer* and the *Journal of the NACGT* in 1992. Watts traced the basis of careers guidance from the liberal welfare tradition at the beginning of the twentieth century to the post-war movement towards greater equality through the 1960s ideas of personal freedom. He observed the irony that it was the very different political philosophy of the 'new right' which had done most to bring guidance close to the top of the policy agenda. He discerned three main strands of 'new right' influence: using guidance as a form of social control, as a means of making markets work and making guidance services themselves more responsive to market forces. By developing this analysis and relating to examples, Tony Watts did much to help members of the Careers Service make sense of what was going on around them, to marshal their arguments and to use their own experience to moderate the policy they were called upon to apply.

A fascinating echo from the 1970s was also made available at about the same time. Windy Dryden and Tony Watts produced *Guidance and Counselling in Britain* (Dryden and Watts 1991), a collection of articles chosen from the *British Journal of Guidance and Counselling* during the 20 years of its existence. Ken Roberts and Peter Daws each recalled their 1977 papers 'The Social Conditions, Consequences and Limitations of Careers Guidance' and 'Are Careers Education

Programmes in Secondary School a Waste of Time?: an Answer to Roberts'. Dryden and Watts point out that, in his postscript, Roberts argued that the introduction of schemes and courses confirmed his view that opportunities rather than personal choice were the strongest determinants of careers. Daws, however, argued that focusing on groups such as unqualified school leavers had resulted in initiatives which did not imply acceptance of the status quo. Roberts and Daws had not changed their respective positions.

It is doubtful whether the policy-makers were listening. Their concern was with governance: with what was best administrated within the structure of the current political framework. If they had a theoretical base, it was probably set within Alec Rodger's work in the 1950s: a rationale rather than a theory of occupational choice.

Chapter 4

1994–2000 careers companies

In July 1993, the new Under Secretary of State, Ann Widdecombe, who impressed heads of Careers Service with her rapid grasp of a difficult brief, launched a 'Careers Service Prospectus' seeking bids to provide the Careers Service in 13 selected 'Pathfinder' areas in England. She did so against an awkward background. The government's expenditure plans for 1993–4 and 1995–6 referred to providers as including private companies, TECs, LEAs and the Employment Service. Arrangements would be made in the interim to pay local authorities for administering the Service, under direction from the Department of Employment.

There were doubts about whether there was enough money to run the service under the new arrangements in the light of curbs in public expenditure. Coopers and Lybrand and Eversheds, acting as consultants, had raised questions over the transfer of assets and the payment of VAT and Corporation Tax. There was general concern about the transfer of undertakings to existing employees (TUPE). The Careers Service Consultative Group considered postponing the change until the position became clearer but rejected the possibility. The government was determined to stick to its plan.

An announcement of thirteen 'pathfinder' areas was followed by the issue of Requirements and Guidance for Providers (DE 1993a) which specified the service the Department would require of contractors once the 1993 Act came into force in April 1994. It also replaced *The Careers Service: Guidance for LEAs* (1974) as the basis on which 'directed' services (those continuing to be run temporarily by LEAs acting under the direction of the Secretary of State) would operate for the time being.

The legislative and administrative structure of the new Careers Service was now quite clear. The service was to operate under The Trade Union Reform and Employment Rights Act 1993, through arrangements specified in Chapter 19, Part III, Sections 45 and 46. This chapter replaced the requirements of Sections 8–10 of the Employment and Training Act 1973 (that LEAs must provide Careers Services), with a duty for the Secretary of State for Employment to ensure the provision of a Careers Service. Specifically 'to secure the provision of guidance and placing services for people attending schools and colleges'. The Act also gives the Secretary of State powers to arrange for the provision of such services for other people.

The *Requirements and Guidance for Providers* (DE 1993a) specified the principles on which the service should be based, the client group, the key outcomes for individual clients and the supporting processes which must be in place. It concentrated upon access, impartiality, raising expectations and achievement, equal opportunities, support from the local community, and collaboration with others. The basis of the Department's contract with potential providers was thus described over 36 carefully written pages.

Most important of all, perhaps, was the acknowledgement of 'the importance of effective careers guidance in raising skill levels and contributing to the prosperity of the country' and that 'individuals' need for guidance has never been greater as the range of learning routes and options widens'.

In the meantime, the Careers Service prepared to deal with a range of practical problems, many concerning service conditions for staff, particularly superannuation and the Transfer of Undertakings (TUPE) arrangements aimed at securing the rights of individuals when public services were privatised. It was established in time that TUPE would apply, allowing existing staff to relax to some extent. Superannuation arrangements remained unclear however. There was talk of setting up a Careers Service scheme, when some county treasurers suggested that employees of the new Careers Services might not remain eligible for the local government scheme.

Elsewhere, a number of other complementary developments were taking place. Cynthia Gittins of Dorset and Terry Collins of Hampshire were working hard to ensure that the putative Industry Lead Body for careers guidance would be as effective as possible. The National Advisory Council for Careers Education and Guidance (foreshadowed in the early days of the Bill) was being set up under the chairmanship of Christopher Ball, with the strong influence of CBI and RSA and with ICG and UK Heads of Careers Service Group as members of the Council.

Most attention was centred upon the 'pathfinder' areas. Well chosen, they represented a variety of areas. Some, like Oldham, Sunderland, Surrey and Bedfordshire, seemed straightforward; others, like the Black Country, were apparently designed to test the opportunity to create a unified service in an area well-known for its variety of local authorities and TECs.

On 28 March 1994, Ann Widdecombe, the Employment Minister, announced the names of the successful pathfinder bidders. They included a range of providers, including an established private provider of education services (Nord Anglia) in Stockport and High Peak, new companies formed for the purpose (in Surrey and North Yorkshire), a range of not-for-profit companies formed by LEAs and TECs and one, the least likely of all perhaps, a single LEA (Bedfordshire).

The Minister was not entirely satisfied, however. Announcing the next round of bidding, she said 'It is important to listen to the market' and mentioned that she would be holding further discussions with potential providers. The areas to be included in the second round of bidding were to be announced in May. The arrangements for London, where there were particular problems, would be announced in September. The government's firm intention to improve the Careers Service was underscored by the Minister's second announcement, however. Expenditure during 1994/95 was to increase to £140 million overall. £34.5 million would be available to fund preparatory work in schools for pupils in Year 9 and Year 10.

This much was clear but preparations for the next round of bidding were confused. 'Listening to the market' consisted of 'holding discussions with' and 'taking soundings from' a range of potential providers but, as many of these meetings were private (often as part of dinners or lunches), the impression given was of a hidden agenda. The actual agenda was probably simply to increase interest from the private sector in the wake of a limited response to the first round but the effect was to heighten tension and encourage mistrust. Rumour and misunderstanding abounded, making life in the Careers Service and in government offices more difficult than it need have been. Confusion was further increased by the sending of nine thousand letters of invitation to express interest to a huge range of individuals and organisations, including District Councils. The author of 'Dick's Diary' (Dick 1996) claimed to know one individual who had received three copies of the same letter and a TEC director whose milkman, having received one, sought advice on what he ought to do with it.

The process was confined to England. Wales had its own distinctive share of confusion. John Redwood, Secretary of State for Wales, had written to Welsh authorities in Autumn 1993 indicating that he would be inviting bids from LEAs and TECs, establishing legal entity partnerships to run the Service from April 1995. In answer to a parliamentary question in Spring 1994, however, he indicated his intention to submit Careers Services to competitive tendering. This produced a difficult atmosphere in Wales, quite unnecessary in view of the eventual outcome. The Scottish Office, meanwhile, kept its own counsel and made it clear that it would not announce its intentions until it was ready.

The exhausting and expensive bidding process went on in England where the announcement of the successful second round of bidders was made on what was, for many, the last working day before Christmas 1994.

Meanwhile, excellent progress was being made in the arrangements for careers work in schools. In May 1994, a White Paper on Competitiveness ('Competitiveness: Helping Business to Win') set out a wider role for the Careers Service in careers education, with an entitlement for all young people aged 11 to 18, focusing on transition points at 13, 15 and 17. Ann Widdecombe put this in perspective at the ICG Annual Conference at Reading (Widdecombe 1994). She stressed that more would be expected of the Service. Careers advisers must raise aspirations among young people, work more closely with teachers, provide information appropriately and make young people more confident that the decisions they were taking were right for them. In summary she said:

1   The Service needs to understand the contribution it can make towards the economic well-being of the nation and of all of us as individuals.
2   Careers Services will have a new culture, operating in a more businesslike environment.
3   The quality standards will be extremely demanding.

This seemed to set out the whole basis of how careers education and guidance in schools was to be seen. The process was to continue to be a joint effort but much stronger than before.

The Institute of Careers Guidance and the National Association of Careers and Guidance Teachers had been working closely together for some time and had produced 'Certain to Succeed' (ICG/NACGT 1994), setting out the conditions for effective careers work in schools and colleges, and what would be required for success. A great deal of consultation, formal and informal, was taking place. *Better Choices* (DE 1984a), issued jointly by Michael Portillo and Gillian Shephard, Secretaries of State for Employment and Education respectively, was issued setting out the entitlement and naming the main partners as schools, colleges, Careers Services, TECs and LEAs. The entitlement, together with a clear right of access to schools for careers advisers (an important item missing from the TURER Act), acquired the force of legislation through the Education Act.

Meanwhile, the wider field of career guidance was also being strengthened by the creation of the National Council for Careers and Educational Guidance (known as the Guidance Council) and seen by many as the best hope for improving careers guidance for adults. The council had brought to the table professional associations, employers' organisations, education and training institutions, and many more. Its period of gestation had begun in the early days of the TURER Bill at the ICG Annual Conference of 1992 and through the efforts of Stephen McNair of UDACE. Christopher Ball of RSA, Bryan Nicholson of the CBI and Tony Watts of NICEC had played major roles in lobbying the government and setting up the preliminary steering committee. A new industry-lead body for guidance was also created. Cynthia Gittins of Dorset and Terry Collins of Hampshire were also influential in its development.

The 12 months between April 1995 and April 1996 were to be momentous for the Careers Service. This year marked the completion of the whole process by which the government of the day and the permanent civil service which operates its policies achieved the Careers Service it wanted and needed: an important piece of the jigsaw of economic, social and educational services necessary to enable society and government to operate smoothly in the decade which would include the new millennium. Speaking to the ICG/Heads of Careers Service Conference for senior managers in April 1995, James Paice, the new minister responsible, described the Service as 'an essential part of the machinery we need to forge a strong and flexible labour force for Britain.' He acknowledged careers education and guidance as of 'paramount importance to young people, businesses and the national economy.' He claimed that the Service had been 'developing an independence and professionalism over and above the standards achieved prior to the 1993 legislation' (Paice 1995: 20).

During the year, 42 Careers Services were provided under the contract, the remainder by LEAs working under direction. Many had been formed by LEAs and TECs working in partnership, five by private sector companies. The private providers included: CfBT (The Centre for British Teachers), which had previously worked largely in supplying teachers of English as a foreign language and in running inspection services; Nord Anglia, a similar company which also operated some private schools; and Careers Enterprise, formed by Surrey Careers Service Ltd and Partnerships UK.

The complicated situation in London was also about to be resolved, with the final round of competitive tendering to be completed in April 1996. Scotland had taken a separate line. The Scottish Secretary, Lord James Douglas Hamilton, had seen close partnership working between education authorities and Local Enterprise Councils and invited the formation of formal partnerships to run Careers Services on a preferred bidder basis. He was not dogmatic about the legal entity required but preferred companies limited by guarantee. In the interim LEAs were to continue to run the service under direction. Only in cases where no partnership agreement could be reached would there be competitive tendering. In the event this occurred only in Tayside and Fife but, even here, faced with the likelihood of bids from Nord Anglia, CfBT and others, in-house bids were prepared and were eventually successful. The eventual outcome in Scotland, therefore, was provision of the Careers Service in a uniform pattern. The only untidy arrangement was in Strathclyde – the largest local authority area in Europe – where six 'shell companies' were formed but staff remained in LEA employment, leaving LECs feeling marginalised and uncomfortable.

The Secretary of State for Wales also decided against competitive tendering. Partnership companies were formed in Cardiff, Vale, Clwyd, Dyfed, Gwent, Mid Glamorgan, Gwynedd, South West Wales and Powys.

The government finally had the Careers Service it required throughout the United Kingdom. These changes in administration were not unique to the Careers Service of course. As Valerie Bayliss had put it in 1994, 'We are a small part of a widespread revolution that is going on in the way public services are provided across the whole of the industrial world' (Bayliss 1994: 10). Contracting was the foundation of this revolution. The Careers Service, as Howard Davis of the School of Public Policy at the University of Birmingham pointed out, 'is the latest in a long line of public services now being subjected to the fundamental nature of this change' (Davis 1995). Davis saw the advantages brought by contracting as a raised profile in its own right and, more generally:

- An increased focus on service definition.
- An increased focus on service performance.
- An increased clarity of responsibilities.
- An increased emphasis on the right to manage.
- An increased focus on customers.

He was concerned, however, that 'selflessness' might have been undermined and that decisions might not always be made solely in the public interest. He warned also of increased complexity, reduced flexibility and a threat to long-term planning where contractors had no guarantee of contract renewal. Management, staff and clients could suffer as a result.

It was target setting and action planning which caused the first and continuing problem for Careers Service companies. The Treasury's enthusiasm for 'counting beans' put pressure on DfEE to provide a quantitative formula to demonstrate improvement. But setting targets and counting action plan forms was hardly a suitable measure of the quality of guidance offered and led to widespread frustration and strained relationships. There was a genuine question of conscience here. Percy Walton put it neatly when, called back from retirement to talk to Heads of Service in May 1994, he described career guidance in terms of 'tolerating ambiguity'. Early 'injection' models of operation had not worked. One must wait until the client was ready. This approach contrasted sharply with a requirement to record the 'output' of each interview.

But this too was part of a wider picture. Contracting management theory and the view of the new utility of education combined in a passion for measurement in the mid-1990s. Richard Hoggart, in *The Way We Live Now* (Hoggart 1995), describes the application of performance indicators on the work of university lecturers as part of a similar process: 'How could they take into account the fact that good teachers have their best influence by intuition, brilliant insights, patience with individuals, so that their impact becomes immeasurable' (1995: 39). Careers advisers felt similarly constrained.

There were excesses too in the fashionable application of some aspects of corporate culture by Careers Service companies. Some had chosen obscure names so far removed from 'Careers' that they were in danger of misleading their less sophisticated clients and rendering themselves difficult to locate. There was a danger that the national 'Careers Service brand' would disappear. The phrase 'commercial: in confidence', used elsewhere as a defence against industrial espionage, was applied indiscriminately to cover planning and policy documents, forecasts and service level agreements. John Killeen and Jennifer Kidd noted this as a trend when they wrote of the new Careers Service in 1996: 'Worryingly – the new competitive culture seems likely to have the effect of making services wary of sharing ideas about new management and models of practice, fearing that this could strengthen competitors' bids and so lead to the loss of the next contract' (Killeen 1996: 16).

There was a poignancy in the coincidental deaths of the three highly influential honorary secretaries of ICG. Herbert Heginbotham, Ray Hurst and Percy Walton died within a three-month period in 1995. Some of the values they had espoused seemed to be in danger. Certainly some careers advisers felt their own ideals threatened, including some who were consequently lost to the Service.

In general, however, the Careers Service adapted well to the new framework. Heads of Careers Service had, for many years, been leaders in promoting training for senior managers, often using tutors experienced in industry and commerce. Many, when appointed as chief executives of careers companies, were well able to put this training into practice. The revolution had produced a Careers Service able to respond to changes in public policy. By the end of 1995, it was apparent that there was an urgent need for it to do so.

In the best-selling *The State We're In* (Hutton 1995), Will Hutton described a working population divided into three segments: one, consisting of unemployed people registered or unregistered and amounting to 30 per cent, he described as absolutely disadvantaged to such an extent that children in these families were not always well fed. The second, also of 30 per cent, consisted of those working in part-time or full-time badly paid jobs, usually on fixed-term contracts. The third segment of up to 40 per cent consisted of full-time workers who had held their jobs for more than two years and part-time workers who had held their jobs for more than five years. Their market power had increased as that of the others had decreased ever since 1979.

Hutton described how this segmentation was shaping Britain's society, with social security spending a national problem and one in three children directly affected by poverty. He was concerned not only with greater inequality between work-rich and work-poor families, but also with the loss of entrepreneurial flair, productivity and inventiveness which could follow: 'defensive thinking' could become the norm. The opportunity for the newly reorganised Careers Service was readily apparent. Helping people make decisions wisely and showing them how to make systems work for them could directly help to redress disadvantage and contribute to a more productive labour market and a happier society (Peck 1995).

While the Careers Service had been shaken by the upheaval of privatisation, it was still largely in the hands of those who had run it previously. Professional ethics and values remained intact. Central control had been much strengthened by tightly written contracts, but the new Department for Education and Employment now had a heavy stake in the new Service and was keen to demonstrate success. The Careers Service budget had been successfully protected, the contribution to Careers Education, training for teachers and careers information had been strengthened. There was an opportunity to make the Service responsible for co-ordinating careers advice for adults and getting better value from the complex network of short-term initiatives which were so confusing to clients and providers alike. What was needed was a strengthened Careers Service Branch in DfEE and a period of stability underpinned by longer contracts for the new Careers Service companies. A closer working relationship between the head of Careers Service Branch and the chief executives was emerging rapidly, promising further improvement in the future.

The opportunities were evident to policy-makers at the newly merged Department for Education and Employment. Valerie Bayliss, Director of Youth and Education Policy, described the change in terms of the opportunity it offered to achieve a coherent policy for careers education and guidance. She saw the need to bridge the gap between academic and vocational education, promote closer links between business and education, and encourage the principle of lifelong learning. She saw independent and objective careers education and guidance as vital, an entitlement for all young people, including (or maybe, in particular) those with special needs, the disaffected and those leaving care or custody.

Not everyone was so sanguine. Ken Roberts, now Professor of Sociology at the University of Liverpool, from where he had been an acute observer and commentator on the Careers Service since 1968, expressed reservation about the careers service companies: 'Providing guidance on a market basis is not new, but no country in the world runs its mainstream guidance service in this way. It won't work' (Roberts 1995). He was dubious also about the entitlements, 'Virtually the same as services were providing in the 1970s', and targets: 'Not a step forward. It is back to basics with a vengeance.'

John Killeen and Jennifer Kidd (Killeen 1996) warned of the threat to careers advisers' exercise of discretion in their work posed by tighter performance measurement in the form of action plans, and a consequent threat to the profession. They felt that a stronger business ethic would prevail in future, and that competition would make services wary of sharing ideas.

This concern was echoed by two former chairs of the Heads of Careers Services Association, who called for an end to the use of the term 'commercial: in confidence', pointing out that much of the success of the Careers Service in the past had been due to the sharing of ideas. Sharing could also contribute to the formation of policy (Eastwood 1995). They went on to stress opportunities provided by what appeared to be political consensus between Tony Blair's view of a society in which all have a chance to work and prosper through their careers, and the very similar views of the Conservative government. They also recognised the threat to professionalism defined by Killeen and Kidd and called for the Institute of Career Guidance to seek wider, well-qualified membership and become the conscience of the Careers Service. Allister McGowan, the incoming President of ICG, drew close attention to the loss of duality between the Department and LEAs under the new arrangements, calling for a chartered institute to help fill the gap and to counter 'the worst manifestations of a too distant, centralised, bureaucracy driven approach' (McGowan 1995).

Some of these observations were made in response to an invitation by the Director of Youth and Education Policy to join the process of refining the new arrangements. Valerie Bayliss made it clear that the Department was already looking towards the Careers Service as it ought to look in five or ten years' time. She quoted Graham Greene, 'There is always one moment when the door opens and lets the future in.' That moment would be the 1 April 1996. There seemed no doubt that the new structure, which would finally fall into place on that date, would provide the framework within which the Careers Service would improve and evolve for the foreseeable future.

There was some expectation within the Careers Service that a future Labour or Labour/Liberal Democrat government would wish to make some changes, but that these would be on the basis of refining and improving the still-new structure.

There were no Labour Party policy statements in existence at the beginning of 1996 but David Blunkett, the Shadow Secretary of State, was known to have a particular interest in careers education and guidance. His own children were in school, making decisions about subject choice with the help of careers officers. He was well briefed by Sheilagh Wooliscroft, the Head of the Careers Service in Sheffield. His local Labour Party contacts, for example in Shropshire, where Derek Woodvine, Chair of Education Committee was in close touch, kept him up to date.

Blunkett, aware of the width of his brief, was cautious about over-involvement and left consultation to Stephen Byers, a senior member of his team. Byers too was well-informed: coming from a Tyneside constituency where the Careers Service was strong, he had been closely involved as a councillor. It was he who had been credited with the remark 'What the Careers Service must have is the cure for which there is no known illness,' made during the debate on the TURER Act. Byers was the leader of the Labour working group which, with Ruth Gee, former Chair of the Association of College Principals, was due to produce an interim paper entitled 'A Successful Career' but better known as the 'Byers Gee Report'.

Some found it difficult to get close to Byers. He seemed well protected by political advisers. But in February 1996, he met Cathi Bereznicki and Allister McGowan of ICG to discuss the whole question of careers guidance in the UK. Their discussion was largely about the changing nature of lifelong learning and the function of careers guidance in helping to provide continuity, connection and direction. On the new arrangements for the Service, they mentioned the expensive contracting process, problems of staff commitment and difficulties in the purchaser/provider arrangements. But Labour was in listening mode; no policy was revealed. Both David Blunkett and Stephen Byers had intended that a policy statement would be made before the general election, but the Byers Gee document remained incomplete and firmly under wraps. It was never published, but emerged in August 1997 when it was circulated to interested bodies by the Guidance Council.

The report opened with a statement that learning does not pay the dividend it should unless it is linked with guidance 'accessible throughout life' (Byers 1995). The Careers Service was to be 'at the centre of a network of providers' including schools, further education, the Employment Service and individual companies. Staff of the Service were to be given additional training and were to provide an entitlement to adults to have a meeting with an adviser every two years. Close working relationships with the Employment Service were envisaged, so that placing work could be closely integrated with careers planning.

The importance of targeting young people who had fallen out of the system was mentioned. Careers education and guidance were to be better integrated and schools encouraged to appoint senior teachers to co-ordinate the work. There were to be local partnerships. Closer collaboration between the Careers Service and providers of guidance in further and higher education would mean existing resources were used more effectively.

Where management of the service was concerned, the paper mentioned 'a number of unfortunate consequences of the 1993 TURER Act,' but was not specific. It proposed the replacement of contracting by licensing and franchising from 1999. Performance indicators and quality assurance should be streamlined. A national logo was to be introduced. There was a mention of 'local learning forums', and greater regional accountability.

The paper lacked clarity and coherence. It was unfinished. The general thrust of Labour Party policy before the election is clear, however: an all-age Careers Service should be at the centre of careers guidance policy and make a significant contribution to the wider learning and skills agenda from that position.

By the time Stephen Byers spoke to the ICG Annual Conference in September 1996, Labour Party policy, while retaining the basis laid down in the Byers Gee report, had become more rather than less confused. Speaking on 'The Opposition View' (Byers 1995), Byers claimed that the government's view of the Careers Service remained unaltered. He went on to stress the need for guidance throughout life, acknowledge the economic value of guidance and the part identified for it in the three major Labour Party policy documents on lifelong learning, the skills revolution and youth training.

He criticised government policy, claiming that privatisation had compromised impartiality and quality, had been costly and largely cosmetic. A Labour government would look at other models and develop an 'integrated advice system', but there would be 'no turning the clock back'. His confusion became more apparent as he looked at the various elements of the work of the Service. Where schools were concerned, he appeared to believe that, given more time for careers education in the curriculum and freedom from 'local management of schools', schools would be in a good position to provide impartial guidance for pupils up to and including career action planning. This would free careers advisers to provide advice for people of all ages 'in need of a professional service'.

Labour would then transform the way the Benefits Agency, the Employment Service and the revamped Careers Service would work together. He went on to talk about adult guidance as a general need and to ask 'Am I right in thinking there should be a second GP service for learning and work?'. He finished by saying that his thinking was still developing and that the Institute's views would be welcome. Some of his audience were alarmed that his thinking had already advanced so far on the basis of such fragile knowledge of the field.

More detailed policy emerged from an article by Bridget Prentice, MP for Lewisham, in *Careers Guidance Today* at the end of 1996, making the same general points about guidance throughout life and the categorical statement 'An incoming Labour Government will use the Careers Service to maximise the economic benefits of change and transformation in Britain's economy into the twenty-first century' (Prentice 1996: 10). She was similarly forthright on the ways in which the Service would be fundamentally reformed: 'We will refocus and rename it as a Personal Development and Guidance Service. We will retain the statutory responsibility for careers education and guidance, but require LEAs, in partnership with other agencies, to deliver a high quality service.'

Each young person between the ages of 14 and 18 was to have an interview each year. Schools were to prepare pupils for decision-making and career action planning. The new Service could then become more effective in producing job information and would be free to work more with adults. There was some emphasis throughout the article on ensuring that those who were not in work should be studying full-time and that the service should 'target' groups in particular need, such as 'the disappeared'. She said 'If we are serious about everyone having a stake in society, we need to involve these alienated youngsters and give them the support and guidance which will help them decide their future' (Prentice 1996: 10).

Alan Davies, the Head of Careers Branch during the implementation of the 1993 TURER Act, was fond of saying that there were two things in life which one should not see being made. One was sausage, the other policy. The mixture which was Labour policy was beginning to take shape but it promised to make a strange kind of sausage. There was also some suspicion among careers advisers and some members of the boards of Careers Service companies that those stirring this policy mixture were political advisers with their own agenda.

Meanwhile, the Conservative government was busily putting its policy into practice and demonstrating commitment to the Careers Service. 'Shaping the Future' (DfEE 1996), the first conference for chairs and chief executives of Careers Service companies, held in an expensive hotel near Heathrow, attracted 200 delegates. Linda Ammon, the able and enthusiastic head of Careers Division, was able to parade Gillian Shephard, the Secretary of State, Michael Bichard, the Permanent Secretary and four DfEE directors. Gillian Shephard's theme was the importance of careers guidance to the economy. Tony Watts, another speaker, picked out the importance to the individual of easily available, sustained opportunities for guidance.

Delegates were impressed, although one pointed out that the 'atmosphere of mild euphoria cloaked the fact that Gillian Shephard had ruled out additional resources for work with adults' (Chubb 1996: 2). There was criticism of the contracting system, and a feeling that the new companies were expected to be more efficient than previously but without a definition of what this might mean. The issues identified for further discussion in the future were:

- An agreement by the Department to re-examine the contracting process.
- A national body to represent Careers Services.

- The national image of the Service.
- Adult guidance.

Shortly afterwards, the Careers Service National Association, which had replaced the UK Heads of Careers Service Group, widened its structure to include chairmen of companies and became the national representative body. Chief executives generally felt relief and increasing confidence in the future.

In May, the Institute of Careers Guidance set up a select committee arising out of their annual conference for senior managers to examine the detail of the contract. An ex-president, Paul Chubb, chaired the group, which recommended greater flexibility, improved quality control and audit. They made a point of the need for more time and resources to deal with disadvantaged clients.

The dialogue between the Service, or 'Services' as it was fashionable to call them (plurals were endemic, many individual services using them, as in 'Shropshire Careers Services Ltd') and Choice and Careers Division was improving rapidly. The new Choice and Careers Division felt itself part of the Service, sharing responsibility for success and continual improvement. The head of Division, Linda Ammon used a dynamic, open style, which was exemplified in a frank description of the Division and the work of its staff, published to mark its first birthday in November 1996 (DfEE 1995/6).

Covering careers information, career education, contracting and planning, quality assurance and staff development, her team benefited from a range of senior and experienced members, including John Wilkins, a seasoned administrator, Peter Heavyside, the Chief Inspector, and John Harradance, the Principal Psychologist. The prospect for positive influence on future policy seemed bright. Some senior managers felt concern that the regional government offices appeared less competent and less sympathetic. If there was some strain between the centre and the regions, that would not be surprising: there was a good deal of talk about regionalism in general. But the new and potentially powerful DfEE was still finding its feet and the Careers Service was seen as an important part of the 'merger bonus'.

The 1996 Dearing Report held the prospect of further fundamental change. Ron Dearing made proposals, including a national qualifications framework; work or college placements for some 14-year-old pupils; A/S Levels, and a re-launch of Youth Training. Careers guidance and the Careers Service featured strongly. Later, the House of Commons Education Select Committee suggested setting up local careers forums, and the DfEE Permanent Secretary talked of the Careers Service as something which had always been a partnership between central and local government. The new Careers Service was becoming a focus of educational interest. Articles exploring its potential contribution appeared in the *Local Government Chronicle* (Peck 1996) and *Careers Guidance Today* (Peck 1996). The debate ranged around the way local Careers Service companies might use their independent position to run local training, education and employment councils to bring together TECs, local authorities and schools, colleges and the Employment Service. Reporting to regional boards, serviced by the DfEE regional directors, such bodies could provide DfEE with planning advice on employment policy and education and training provision. They could have become regional learning and skills councils.

In retrospect, these ideas might seem far fetched. They did not seem so in the run-up to the general election of 1997. The Conservative view of the Service remained optimistic and enthusiastic. Raymond Robertson, MP, had spoken of the recent reforms thus: 'Bringing educationalists and business people together to run Careers Services has been good news'; and 'You should not doubt the Government's commitment to the Careers Service' (Robertson 1996). And while the Labour Party's position was less clear due to Stephen Byers' ambiguous presentation and Bridget Prentice's confusing article, this concern was eased to some extent by a meeting between ICG officers and Labour Party representatives in February 1997. Byers' background as AMA Education Chairman, David Blunkett's high reputation and Tony Blair's personal experience were reassuring.

After the election, one of David Blunkett's early duties as Secretary of State was to accept the Chief Inspector's report on the Careers Service for the year ending 1997. He did so, describing Careers Services as central to the changes he wished to make in raising young people's aspirations, the New Deal and in building on partnerships so that Careers Services could fulfil their unique role at the interface between education and employment. 'I have no doubt about the pivotal role of the Careers Service' (DfEE 1997b: 3), he said in his closing paragraph.

The announcement of Labour's Education and Employment Team after the May 1997 General Election victory did little to reassure the Careers Service about its place in the new government's policy. There was a good deal of faith in the Secretary of State, David Blunkett, of course. He had made clear throughout the campaign that Labour would issue a policy document on careers guidance at some stage. This was confirmed shortly after the election when he spoke to the Careers Service National Association in June. It seemed sensible, therefore, to wait for the paper to appear but it never did.

It was the make-up of his team and the division of responsibility between ministers which cast doubt upon the likelihood of a central role for the Careers Service. Employment policy, and especially the New Deal, had been a major issue during the election. Responsibility for this went to Andrew Smith, Minister for Employment, making it apparent that the Employment Service would take the central role, leaving the Careers Service to provide support. This seemed to confirm the position of the Careers Service as a 'youth service', confined largely to those under 18, rather than a putative all-age guidance service.

The minister with responsibility for the Careers Service was to be Tessa Blackstone, brought in from the House of Lords to run a huge portfolio, including higher education, examinations across the board, youth training and public services reform. Her career in higher education and, previously, as an administrator in the Inner London Education Authority seemed relevant. Her reputation amongst careers advisers, however, was as someone who was generally sceptical about careers advice, questioning its necessity, especially for those from a good family background with high academic ability who could be well serviced by school careers education programmes alone. Where adults were concerned, she was interested in a wide range of bodies offering educational and careers advice to those seeking to enter higher education and training. Her parliamentary under secretary was Kim Howells, whose direct responsibilities included the youth service, Training and Enterprise Councils and public/private partnerships.

Any reform of the administrative or policy framework of the Careers Service began to seem unlikely and this impression was reinforced by the Department's consultation document *Learning and Working Together for the Future* (DfEE 1997) produced later in 1997. This paper represented the civil servants' interpretation of the new government's wishes and how they would be put into practice. David Blunkett's foreword stressed 'economic competitiveness' and 'social cohesion' (1997: 1). The DfEE, 'with the Employment Service', was seen as being at the centre of this ambitious agenda for change and renewal. The Careers Service, despite its potential to play a wider role, was not mentioned. Nor, as the ICG chief executive pointed out, were the economic value of careers guidance or the impartiality of careers advisers. The ICG response was to stress the importance of careers education and guidance, the need for a better framework for guidance for adults and the potential for careers advisers to work as 'key workers', referring clients to other specialist services where necessary (ICG 1997).

When Baroness Blackstone addressed the ICG Conference in 1997 she took a broad view, ranging over the possibility of joint training of careers officers and teachers, the importance of the later years in primary schools, and the integration of careers education into the curriculum. She talked of 'inclusion' and of the need to spend more time attending to the needs of the 'socially excluded'. But she did not deal with the specific concerns of careers advisers. Subsequent attempts to arrange a meeting between ICG officers and government ministers failed. The impression gained was that ideas were being discussed elsewhere, but no one was ready to talk to the Careers Service about them.

More emerged from a speech by Kim Howells made to the second Annual Careers Service Companies Conference at a Heathrow hotel on 3 November 1997 (Howells 1997). He described the six challenges to the Department as: raising standards, tackling social exclusion, welfare to work, creating partnerships, lifelong learning and a flexible labour market. While he stressed the need for partnerships with schools, TECs and the Employment Service, he focused on young people, particularly those who had 'dropped out'. 'By refocusing your efforts, you can help us address this ambitious agenda,' he said. Dr Howells mentioned his pride in the 'comprehensive system of careers education in this country.' His speech aimed at spelling out the role of the Careers Service for the rest of this parliament. The Careers and Occupational Information Centre's 'Newscheck' on 3 December reported the speech, and a subsequent address at an evening reception by Baroness Blackstone, under the heading 'ministers demonstrate support for the Careers Service' (DfEE 1997).

The pride in the achievements of the Careers Service which Kim Howells and David Blunkett had each expressed in the short period since the election and their apparent intention to leave the existing arrangements in place had meanwhile been reinforced by the report of the National Audit Office 'Contracting out of Careers Services in England' issued in July 1997 (DfEE 1997c). While the report criticised the 'costly contracting out mechanism', it judged that the first objective – providing competition, commercial freedoms and flexibility and exposing providers to private sector disciplines – had essentially been achieved. The other objectives of ensuring that high standards were achieved everywhere, responding better to local circumstances and securing closer involvement of employers, had shown substantial progress. Kim Howells' use of the word 'refocusing', however, was perhaps the first indication of a fundamental change in the policy remit of the Careers Service.

There had been concern amongst careers advisers for many years about young people who had become 'disengaged'. Careers Services locally and nationally had developed a number of initiatives to deal with their problems. The European Social Fund-financed Youthstart Mentoring Action Programme (known as MAP) was the largest and most successful.

The project concentrated on training and supporting careers advisers working with this broadly defined group or, in some cases, particular groups such as young mothers, college drop-outs, early school leavers and young offenders. It was managed by the Institute of Career Guidance, working in collaboration with 20 Careers Service companies.

Lyn Barham, the consultant who created and developed the project while working with the Institute, remembered that the concept was so radical that it was described at its launch as subversive, in the best sense that it reminded everyone, including the government of the day, of the importance of this element of careers work. The Labour government's 'New Start' project followed this lead by funding 17 local partnerships designed to draw together existing work. The early days of the 'New Deal Gateway' also made good use of careers advisers' skills and helped them gain experience.

There were other signs of developing concepts of careers work as Tony Watts began to write and talk about 'Careerquake' (Watts 1997) (the rapidly changing world of work) and the Royal Society of Arts published two items arising from its 'Redefining Work' project: *Key Views on the Future of Work* (Bayliss 1997) and *The Internal Labour Market* (Simpson 1997). The Institute of Careers Guidance held a 'Year of Careers Guidance', celebrating 1997 as the year in which a professional association of careers advisers reached its seventy-fifth birthday.

While the emphasis of Careers Service work was evolving under the still-new regime of the Careers Service companies and their relationship with the DfEE, a more fundamental change of policy was in the mind of the new government. From 1993–97 the basis of the contracts between the Department and careers companies had been on the numbers and quality of young peoples' action plans emerging from careers interviews in schools and elsewhere. Some felt there was too much emphasis on counting and that careers advisers were sometimes pressed into recording premature decisions so as to meet their targets. But the principle remained clear: there was an equal entitlement for all young people. What lay in the minds of the new government ran contrary to this principle. 'Refocusing' or focusing as it came to be known was based on the belief that some young people needed more help than others in order to make a satisfactory move from school to work.

In practice, young people with problems or special needs had always received extra help from the Careers Service, either through a variety of initiatives to promote outreach (the appointment of unemployment specialist careers officers in the 1980s is a good example and the Youthstart project the most recent) or through the natural concern of careers advisers to keep a close eye on those likely to find difficulty in making the transition to work or extended education. But the principle of universality had always been acknowledged. Earlier local decisions to regard, say, students in selective schools as unlikely to have difficulty in choosing careers, had been shown to be hazardous. Career problems, it was recognised, were not confined to those of low ability or who lacked support from home.

Interestingly, the Youth Service was also being given clear instructions on 'targeting the disaffected'. Bernard Davies (1999) points out that this, the result of Labour's wish to tackle inequality, was nevertheless 'based on societal perspectives and analysis which had serious limitations'. He maintained, however, that it was made clear that extra funding, or the establishment of a firm legislative base for the Youth Service, depended on co-operation with this policy. His summary of the problem for the Youth Service could apply equally to the Careers Service: 'Targeting could end up tipping the centre of gravity away from excitement at young people's possibilities, to anxiety about their inadequacies'.

The new policy became explicit for the Careers Services when it appeared in the 1998 revision of 'Requirements and Guidance for Careers Services'. In his foreword the Secretary of State stressed that: in future, the Careers Service should focus attention on those who need help most, going on to specify increasing expectations and avoiding dropping out, bringing back into learning those in danger of losing their way. The section on principles referred to social inclusion and Careers Services focusing their help on those who are disadvantaged, and for whom it can make the greatest difference.

Careers advisers had a dilemma. Whilst acknowledging the principle, they nevertheless saw the dangers implicit in a sudden change of tack. Their individual focus had been on those *they* judged to be most in need. They feared for their relationship with schools, where they had established ways of working which included referrals from a range of teachers who would now be unlikely to accept that priorities should be changed to the detriment of some pupils. Careers advisers felt responsibility for 'their' schools and caseloads. Instructions to focus their efforts diminished their area of judgement, threatened their relative autonomy and hence their reputation and standing in schools.

At the 1998 ICG Annual Conference, the outgoing president, Stevie Martin, pledged that the Institute would defend the principle of a universal entitlement to guidance, which was seen as potentially, if not actually, being compromised by the current emphasis on focusing on particular groups of clients. The chances of resolving the problem were not good. The Careers Service faced the prospect of being forced to make decisions which virtually withdrew careers advisers from important areas of school work, or of leaving careers advisers to decide for themselves how best to muddle through.

During June 1998, DfEE's Choice and Careers Division held a series of five regional workshops with the title 'Taking Forward Careers Service Focusing'. Their report illustrated the practical difficulties which were emerging under four main headings:

- Identifying individuals in the focus target group.
- Differentiating services to maintain the entitlement.
- Internal management.
- Managing relationships with partners.

A number of wider issues emerged, largely connected with the DfEE contract, including: accounting for work with the disaffected, developing organisations and staff, reviewing finance, sustaining partnerships, and reconsidering relationships between DfEE, its government offices in the regions and local Careers Services.

A Review of Careers Service Focusing in Schools (DfEE 2001), published in September 2001, justified the early concern of the Careers Service and demonstrated just how much confusion was caused by this fundamental but hastily implemented change of policy. The report pointed out that it was the efforts of Careers Services which underpinned the sharp rise in post-16 participation rates, and that the more focused approach had led to many other achievements not specifically covered by the study. Having said that, the report notes a decrease of nearly 32 per cent in the number of group sessions and individual interviews provided for students in education. The reduction of resources allocated to work in education amounted to between 15 per cent and 25 per cent overall. In some schools, reductions could be as much as 40 per cent or 50 per cent.

Figures tell only a part of the story. It is from the comments of teachers and careers advisers quoted in the report that some of the less direct and more harmful effects can be gathered. Some reported evidence 'that among students, access to careers guidance and the careers adviser is becoming stigmatised by an association with a poorly achieving, or poorly behaving, minority'. This seems to have been a direct result of the interpretation of DfEE policy which 'consistently emphasises a clear link between students' guidance needs and their ability'. The most common concern expressed by schools was about equal opportunity. Several reported reluctance by some staff to take part in a process to identify those who should receive help. Several Careers Services expressed concern about the effect on multi-cultural communities of the withdrawal of a universal service.

There was general disquiet among careers advisers and their managers about the way refocusing was being handled by DfEE. In particular, there was a sense that those making policy lacked understanding of the work of the Service, despite the recent pronouncement on its economic and social value, and expressions of satisfaction with the way in which the still-new arrangements were working. A new policy required additional resources if it was not to be implemented at the expense of others. There seemed no reason why ministers and advisers should not understand that they could meet some of their educational, economic and social policies through the Careers Service. Some chief executives began to wonder whether DfEE civil servants were well aware of this but uneasy about the growth of the Service and its influence. Perhaps they saw it as the cuckoo in the nest, which did not always fit the reality of the government's actions.

There was also some anxiety about the empty repetition of fashionable words. For example, no ministerial speech or announcement was complete without a mention of 'partnership' as a goal. Careers advisers were already working in partnership with others: many companies were based on partnerships between TECs and LEAs; but here, in refocusing, was a mandatory requirement which was threatening some established partnerships, especially with schools and colleges.

In fact, the experience of Careers Services of working in partnership was probably unrivalled in the public sector, especially in the area of careers guidance for adults. The majority of Services were involved, but largely through using short-term 'funny money' from ESF and SRB projects, specialist funding for groups with particular problems, or work with unemployed people. Almost invariably, these projects were dependent upon local partnerships, usually involving TECs and the Employment Service and often led by the Careers Service.

A survey of Careers Service work with adults carried out by the Centre for Guidance Studies, published in 2001, pointed out that part of the intention of the 1993 TURER Act had been to encourage Careers Service companies to extend services to adults on a fee-paying or separately funded basis. This had not happened quite as expected. A survey by ICG in 1996 (ICG 1996) showed that the initial affect of contracting out was to reduce the number of Services working with adults by one in seven due to lack of funding. Nevertheless, enthusiasm and experience remained high and companies gradually accumulated surpluses which they were able to devote to this area of work. They were, therefore, well placed to respond when, in 1998, the government announced funding of £54 million to be made available for information, advice and guidance services (IAGs) over the years 1999 to 2002. Based on partnerships, including statutory, community and voluntary groups, the IAGs were each to have a lead body. In most partnerships the local careers company emerged as the most suitable partner to fulfil this role.

Chapter 5

2000–2001 Connexions and disconnections

The best start in life for every young person

Concentrating on its own place in the scheme of things, the Careers Service failed to see the wider picture. Seeking to contribute to the government's education and economic policies, especially life long learning, the Service was largely unaware of the way government advisers were pressing their social agenda. Refocusing, seen as an additional task, valuable but threatening to the main career guidance remit, was being seen by advisers as an absolute priority, overriding Labour's pre-election policy contained in the draft Byers Gee report.

In order to put this into context it is necessary to re-examine the broad thrust of Labour policy in 1998/99 and then to review the thinking of influential advisers, who had been working for some time on their own policy solutions to social and economic problems.

The Labour government had come into power with a vision. It would strive for sound economic growth, appealing to business and the middle classes, while also attempting to deal with disadvantage. In planning for young people it felt itself on safe ground. Here were no difficult questions of whether they were deserving of help; no judgement of their merit was required. All could accept that their education, training and eventual employment were a priority.

Less explicit was the government's view of inequality and its persistence. The differing life chances of young people with low paid parents was demonstrably different from those with highly paid parents: that did not need to be explained. Work was to be at the centre of the policy of inclusion in the new Britain. It was important that all should see its advantages, irrespective of level of income or responsibility for others. Exclusion from work was to be avoided at all cost.

'Social exclusion' was, to some extent, a euphemism for poverty or for 'the underclass', who were in danger of living lives that were generally unsatisfactory, whose cost to the medical and social services was high, and whose contribution to economic and social well-being was negligible.

The concept of social exclusion provided a way of grappling with the situation described by Will Hutton (1995) before the election. It espoused the moral dimension set out frequently by Tony Blair, most notably in his *Spectator* lecture in 1995 (Blair 1995), where he pointed out that 'individuals prosper best within a strong and cohesive society,' and went on to say 'we are entitled to expect responsibility in return for creating opportunities for all.' He saw the need for: 'A culture of responsibility to be embedded in every class and every school.'

Tony Watts (Watts 2001) has pointed out that social exclusion had been a focus of political debate in France since the 1960s and had exercised a growing influence on social and economic policy in the European Union since about 1994. Britain came close to the top of Europe's most undesirable league table in 1997: child poverty, teenage pregnancies, children in homes where no one worked and adult literacy. Small wonder, therefore, that the Blair government found social exclusion a useful concept and that, in 1997, the Prime Minister himself launched the Social Exclusion Unit and appointed Moira Wallace, a civil servant from his own office, to lead it.

The Unit decided to concentrate upon four major areas: rough sleeping, teenage pregnancies, 16–18-year-olds not in education or employment, and neighbourhood renewal. With an agenda as wide as this it is unsurprising that they were concerned with radical change, rather than with relatively minor issues like the further modification of a Careers Service reformed to the requirements of a previous Conservative government. With their own agenda to the fore, the need for joined-up government in their minds, and advice from people like Geoff Mulgan to take into account, the creation of a new service designed to deal with one of their priority areas, and contribute to solutions to others, was bound to appeal.

The announcement of a new Youth Support Service in England came in a White Paper 'Learning to Succeed: A New Framework for Learning' published in June 1999 (DfEE 1999a). This White Paper was based on the ideas first set out in a Green Paper 'The Learning Age', which included lifelong learning partnerships. The main strand of the White Paper's proposals was the establishment of a 'Learning Skills Council for England' to be in place by April 2001. The council's responsibilities were to include the funding of further education colleges, modern apprenticeships, national traineeships and all other government training schemes. Employers were to be closely involved. The council was to operate through 50 local Learning and Skills Councils, which would have sufficient autonomy to allow them to match provision to local needs.

The Youth Support Service was to provide a comprehensive structure for advice and support for all young people from the age of 13 and would be 'a step change in the way support is provided to young people'. The service was to be organised on the same geographical basis as the local Learning and Skills Councils. Significantly, the Careers Service was to have to wait for details of the new service from a subsequent report from the Social Exclusion Unit – *Bridging the Gap*. *Learning to Succeed* named the service 'Connexions', describing it as 'an enhanced strategy for making sure that far more young people continue in education and training until they are at least 19'. The responsibility of the new service was to extend to all young people but it would 'focus on keeping track of the most disadvantaged young people and helping those most at risk of dropping out.'

This much was clear, but confusion followed. There was a reference to improving the coherence of organisations such as the Careers Service, parts of the Youth Service and a range of other specialist agencies. There was reference to the importance of careers information and advice, and that young people should be aware of national and local labour market information. This was followed by an assertion that 'This is an area which has been weak,' which seemed to contradict what David Blunkett and his aides had been saying about the Careers Service in their annual reports.

Perhaps Blunkett himself was apprehensive. He telephoned the Careers Service National Association the evening before *Learning to Succeed* was published, asking them to be prepared to respond to consultations at a later stage. The immediate response of the Service was to underline the need for a universal service, and to stress their involvement in adult as well as 'youth work'.

The time for more detailed reaction was to come with the release of *Bridging the Gap: New Opportunities for 16 Year Olds Not in Education or Training* (DfEE 1999) presented to Parliament by the Prime Minister in July 1999. Most of the 101 pages of *Bridging the Gap* were devoted to brief case studies and examples of how young people fell out of education and training. Not all were good examples, nor did they always meet the cases being made. In essence, the report made the following proposals to keep young people in the system:

1   A new graduation certificate, with a variety of ways to reach graduation.
2   Financial help to keep young people in school, built on education maintenance allowances.
3   A new multi-skilled support service working with all young people, but giving priority to those most at risk of under-achievement and disaffection; to support them between the ages of 13 and 19 through education to adulthood.

This service – ConneXions – spelt here for the first time with a capital 'X' was to:

1   Work with schools to improve preparation for post-16 choices.
2   Provide a full service of advice and support for 13-to-19-year-olds, including personal advisers for those in need of help.
3   Deliver targets for achievement of graduation through work with individual young people and by influencing education and training providers.

But it is not in the body of *Bridging the Gap* that the ideology and politics behind Connexions are to be found. They are there in the Prime Minister's foreword, the beliefs of advisers, especially Geoff Mulgan (described by Tony Watts as the *eminence gris* (Watts 2000)) and in the name itself. The name 'ConneXions' seemed to appear from nowhere. It is difficult to trace its origin. One relatively junior civil servant said firmly, but off the record, that it was 'chosen by young people themselves'. Perhaps this means that it emerged from a focus group or from consultants. It was not mentioned by Careers Branch civil servants to the Careers Service National Association or the Institute of Career Guidance. There was no consultation with chairmen of boards. The name was firmly attached by SEU before consultation or critical opinion could get in the way.

The foreword, well written in plain English, sets out the government's policy clearly. It begins 'The best defence against social exclusion is a job,' and goes on to describe a better life for young people and a better deal for society as a whole: the double dividends provided by falling crime and welfare bills. Tony Watts points out that *Bridging the Gap* had, at an earlier stage, been sent to the DfEE and other departments with the strong personal endorsement of the Prime Minister (Watts 2000). This is entirely credible: it seems to typify Mr Blair's personal beliefs and convictions. The traditions and beliefs of the older Careers Service, which he had previously understood so well, could not be allowed to stand in the way of an apparently more fundamental and revolutionary New Labour approach, which embodied the careful work and beliefs of one of his closest advisers.

Geoff Mulgan had originally been appointed as adviser to the Number 10 Policy Unit. Previously he had been director of Demos, a left-leaning think tank. He was, therefore, well able to influence the work of the Social Exclusion Unit. Mr Mulgan's position on social policy can be seen from his subsequent career. By 2002 he had become Director of the Performance and Innovation Unit of the Cabinet Office. In his words the PIU exists to 'Challenge received wisdom and devise solutions which people own and want to implement' (Wintour 2002). Challenging received wisdom is exactly what the SEU saw itself doing when it produced *Bridging the Gap*.

What is missing from the Social Exclusion Unit's work is any evidence of substantial research, or expert opinion from the careers community, education or employers. ICG, NACGT, NICEC and the Guidance Council were not involved. Probably SEU had access to advice from the youth workers among their advisers, but whether this was representative of the Youth Service and LEAs seems unlikely in the light of the latter's subsequent reaction.

It is difficult to be precise about the theoretical underpinnings of Connexions but reading the literature, analysing the careful commentaries of Tony Watts (Watts 2001) and a number of interviews with those directly concerned (some of whom were prepared to speak only off the record), reveals a nucleus of ideas supported by a number of preconceptions and misconceptions.

The main ideas stemmed from Demos, which had been responsible for *Destination Unknown: Engaging with the Problems of Marginalised Youth* (1999) by Tom Bentley and Ravi Gurumurthy, who in turn drew on the findings of an earlier enquiry into young people's views of government policy and social exclusion: *The Real Deal* (Bentley 1999). The reference and acknowledgement sections of *Destination Unknown* contain almost no mention of the Careers Service. There are passing references made to careers and 'Careers' in the body of the book, but more references are made to the Employment Service. The public service framework overall is regarded as having failed and the privatisation of the Careers Service is given as one reason for the loosening of the infrastructure. The post-16 framework is regarded as 'impossibly fragmented and incoherent'.

The solution to this problem was seen to lie in 'brokerage'. There are references to projects in the USA and Australia, to 'Youthlink' in Surrey, and to 'Youthreach' in Derbyshire. There are many quotations from interviews with young people. There is a good deal about community resources, role models and mentors. But the main recommendation is quite clear: there should be a 'Youth Brokerage Service' and within 10 years there should be a new profession responsible for ensuring coherence based in schools, colleges and youth centres. Available to young people from the age of about 14, the new service could be formed from a merger of the youth, careers and education welfare services.

The Institute of Public Policy Research might also have had some influence at this early stage. They produced *Wasted Youth, Raising Achievement and Tackling Social Exclusion* (Pearce and Hillman 1999). The authors, Nick Pearce and Josh Hillman, were more guarded but made a strong case for focusing on 'status zero' young people and for the eventual integration of local services. They claimed that disaffected young people often viewed the Careers Service with indifference or disdain. There might also have been some input from the DfEE's Careers Service Branch but, for the most part, civil servants seem to have been sidelined, even though they had been impressed by the success of projects such as 'Newstart', 'Base 10' (in Sheffield), and 'Leeds Apex'. Some had retained the concern engendered by the 1993 Audit Commission report about high drop-out rates from further education. Others were uneasy about the still-new careers companies. 'Excellence in Cities', a scheme using mentors in schools in Coventry and a number of cities with similar problems, had created a favourable impression.

But the main idea behind Connexions was that of 'youth broker', easily translated to 'personal adviser'. Someone who could be all things to all young people, a general practitioner who could ensure access to specialists where necessary. The personal adviser/youth broker was seen as someone who would replace the vested interests of existing professionals devoted to the maintenance of institutional boundaries. In fact, there was little evidence of turf wars or professional rivalries. Perhaps this was an echo of Tony Blair's distrust of the 'forces of conservatism' so apparent to him in the health service, education and other public services.

Given the opportunity to contribute their opinions, many youth workers and careers advisers might well have accepted a need for them to work more closely together and for frequent and more careful cross-referral of young people with problems. They would have pointed out, however, their different, if complementary, roles. Both would have stressed their strong, but different, relationships with and to teachers.

There was an ambivalence amongst advisers and ministers about the Careers Service. Perhaps it was the word 'Careers' which gave them a middle-class impression and an over-concern with able, middle-class clients. Baroness Tessa Blackstone, Minister of State in DfEE, was one who gave a strong impression that many existing clients of the Careers Service could look after themselves. Careers advisers would then have time to focus on young people with problems. The ambivalence went further. Some seemed to believe that the Service was ripe for reform, apparently unaware of the TURER reforms of 1994. Others seemed to believe that they would face resistance to further change from a profession newly devoted to the free market principles of the careers companies, the brainchild of the previous Conservative administration.

Also pressing was the need in Whitehall to produce evidence of 'joined-up government' in practice. An opportunity to link new creations like Youth Offending Teams with older bodies like the Youth Service, Education, Welfare and the Careers Service was too good to miss. But the outstanding opportunity was the availability of an already captive budget within DfEE. The careers companies gave the impression of independence but their income where their core business was concerned depended entirely upon the DfEE contract. The Department had control of the purse strings and could distribute money through contracts as it wished. There were no problems of legislation either; the 'Henry the Eighth Legislation' of the TURER Act gave the Department *carte blanche* to carry out its statutory duties as it saw fit. The Careers Service budget was readily available for redirection.

The same was not true of either the Youth Service or Education Welfare. Their operation was bound up with local education authorities, who would not easily give up their influence or their budgets. They had lost their responsibility for the Careers Service only five years before and would not be caught again.

But, while there was no financial obstacle to making the Careers Service into 'Connexions' (or so it seemed), there were valid objections and practical difficulties. 'Joined-up government' did not represent 'joined up guidance': this phrase was coined by Valerie Bayliss, previously Head of Youth Programmes at DfEE. She, Tony Watts of NICEC, the ICG and the Careers Service National Association were quick to respond to the belated opportunity for consultation.

The first general opportunity for careers advisers to discuss the planned revolution in their Service was provided by the Institute of Career Guidance Conference in August 1999. The irony of the situation was not lost on delegates as they gathered in Warwick with members of the International Association of Educational and Vocational Guidance to discuss the wider aspects of their profession. The President, Monica Lemecha, set the tone by talking of achieving chartered status and a register of guidance professionals. Tony Watts contributed an international perspective on career guidance and public policy. John Malkin, the incoming President, pointed out that the strongest body of knowledge about guidance was there in Warwick University's main hall for those few days. No wonder then that the opening session, led by past-president Allister McGowan, had an air of incredulity about it.

Despite their surprise that such radical change had not been indicated before the release of the two reports, members acknowledged some merit in *Learning to Succeed* and *Bridging the Gap*. Their confusion sprang from the government's failure to consider properly the need for an all-age guidance service to underpin lifelong learning. They pointed out that many young people reached the stage of making firm decisions only in their early 20s. An age limit would be against their interests. There was concern also about the ambiguity of the personal adviser role, the prospect of a policing element in education welfare and the dangers of a generic role similar to that which had bedevilled social work practice since the 1970s. Their main concerns were that access should be universal and that the focus should be on 'career', rather than simply 'learning' or 'dropping out'.

The first public response to the government's proposals came from Tony Watts, whose strongly critical article 'Death of Careers' appeared in *The Times Educational Supplement* on 29 October 1999. Watts pointed out that the government seemed poised to dismantle the Careers Service by default and that, while schools, colleges, parents and young people would all be affected, few knew what was happening. He argued that, while a few would be helped, the proposals made no sense where the majority was concerned and that what most students needed was career guidance. Raising achievement and lifelong learning seemed to be neglected under the new proposals, and able students left to fend for themselves. The danger was that, rather than making an extra contribution to young people at risk, the Careers Service would disappear within the new framework.

The second response was similarly important because it came from Valerie Bayliss who had, until recently, been the distinguished senior civil servant with most expertise in guidance and the architect of the recently reformed Careers Service. From her new vantage point as Vice-Chair of the Guidance Council and Professor Associate at the University of Sheffield's Education Studies Department, she gave the annual lecture at the Centre for Guidance Studies at the University of Derby in December 1999. Taking as her theme 'Joined up Guidance: Where Do We Go From Here' (Bayliss 1999), Bayliss described the 1990s as a decade of huge progress, with a much improved Careers Service working more closely with schools as an important part of joined-up career education and guidance, with much more money than before devoted to careers work. While she accepted that many of the reforms under the Major government might have happened by accident rather than the application of consistent policy, she detected a much less secure understanding of the issues and a reluctance to engage in open debate from the Blair government.

Her concerns about the Youth Support Service centred on the government's failure to spell out what the new 'universal' service would do: the much quoted view that the more able would not need career advice; the failure to make proper reference to careers education; the SEU's static analysis of disadvantage; and its restriction to issues outside education. A deficit model for the disadvantaged would not work. It would be a pity, she said, if 'a brave attempt at joined up policy on youth support, in fact, produced the very opposite result' (Bayliss: 1999).

Valerie Bayliss went on to outline an agenda for the guidance community over the whole field of lifelong learning for young people and adults. The debate should cover: the case for guidance; the resourcing of guidance services; guidance to include careers and employment prospects as well as lifelong learning, and consistency of policy across the age range. She concluded that progress might be easier if ways were found to help government, rather than leaving all the thinking to them, and with the hope that the last decade would be remembered not as a high watermark, but as a stepping stone in the recognition that access to high quality guidance for everyone is part of a civilised society.

These interventions from outside the Careers Service gave a strong foundation to the ensuing campaign to modify and improve the policy of a government which had avoided consultation thus far. The Careers Service National Association in particular (they were the contract holders), and the Institute of Careers Guidance (who represented most careers advisers), could have been accused of vested interest if they had rushed to the defence of their own service. Their subsequent response had greater authority, especially as it was to be co-ordinated by the Guidance Council working for the whole guidance community led by Tim Glass, their Chief Executive, and Tony Watts of NICEC.

Official responses to the White Paper and the SEU Report were first discussed at the Institute of Careers Guidance Conference in August 1999 at Warwick. There, a meeting of senior figures in the guidance community, representing the Guidance Council, the Local Government Association, the Careers Service National Association, the Institute and NICEC amongst others, decided that the Guidance Council should produce a common response from all its members, including those mentioned here. Member organisations could also make their own individual responses.

The council's response began by specifying the role which guidance could play in achieving government policy in:

- Reducing social exclusion.
- Raising achievement for all.
- Placing the learner at the centre of the education and training system.
- Increasing participation, retention and progression in education, training and employment.

It suggested that provision should be tested against the full range of these aims. It went on to stress that access to guidance should be universal and lifelong.

Turning to the new Connexions strategy, it welcomed the major thrust, but warned that the way the proposals were framed appeared to be based on a clearly identified group of disaffected young people, whereas there is, in fact, a very volatile group, with people moving in and out constantly. It pointed to the risk of stigmatising the Service, making screening difficult and neglecting career education and guidance for all. It urged the avoidance of unnecessary restructuring, the need to build on local provision and to avoid producing conflicts of role.

To read this paper is to realise just how much the government had lost by its failure to consult earlier in the process. Had ministers had a brief of this quality before them when they framed their White Paper, the chances of successfully translating policy into practice would have been much improved.

The response of the Institute of Career Guidance (ICG 1999) was similarly valuable, with similar principles at its base. It concluded that the government should take its time, learning from the approach in Scotland and Wales, avoiding moving too rapidly in a direction unsupported by sufficient evidence for success. It stressed that local partnership working could avoid the disruption and expense of radical restructuring. In addition, the paper underlined the importance of qualified staff and arrangements such as those contained in its own register of guidance practitioners. It made the case for guidance delivery to be 'all age'. It stressed the point that many young people do not become interested in lifelong learning until their early 20s, and pointed out that access must be universal because lifelong learning is much broader than social exclusion.

The response of the Careers Service National Association (CSNA 1999), as might have been expected, tended to concentrate upon administrative, management and delivery systems. It pointed out that its members could offer solutions that built upon current structures without upheaval, concentrating effort quickly and effectively. It recommended:

- Universal access.
- Tailored support to those most at risk.
- Tracking the whole 13–19 cohort.
- National standards.
- Professional support for schools, colleges and work-based learning.
- Coherence between youth and adult services.

Throughout its response the Association stressed its willingness to work with the government to ensure that the implementation of the proposals might be executed smoothly and effectively.

This is an account of the response of those organisations closest to the Careers Service. Amongst the wider response, however, it is worth noting the informal reaction of the Youth Service. In the year of the sixtieth anniversary of the Service, leaders of the National Youth Agency and the Community and Youth Workers Union accused the government of 'cherry-picking' (Jones 1999). Their fear was of superficiality and that any suggestion of 'conscription' would not entice young people back into formal education. The Youth Service had expected that a Labour government would pass legislation to give it a statutory function. There was no enthusiasm among youth workers for a youth support service which would 'strip local authorities of control and merge it with careers'.

Chapter 6

Diversity and divergence

It was inevitable that the early months of the new millennium would be an anxious time for the Careers Service. As Bryony Pawinska, ICG's Chief Executive, pointed out in the January 2000 edition of *Careers Guidance Today*, 'Many of our members have been living with the anxiety and confusion arising from almost daily changes in speculation about the future' (Pawinska 2000: 2). Some feared that while the consultation in which they were about to be involved might modify the detail, the shape of Connexions was set. Nevertheless, a great deal of energy was put into the task of modifying and improving the proposals. The Guidance Council carried out its lead role conscientiously. It was decided that Tony Watts would prepare a series of policy bulletins to keep members up to date and to allow him and Tim Glass, the Chief Executive, to receive regular comment and feedback.

The first issue, on 8 February 2000, concentrated on the second reading of the Learning and Skills Bill in the House of Lords and the policy document on the Connexions Service *Connexions: The Best Start in Life for Every Young Person*, issued on 3 February, together with a press statement. The press release also announced the first five pilots in Coventry and Warwickshire, Cornwall and Devon, Lewisham, Hampshire, and Humberside.

The government's publicity generally centred on the role of the personal advisers, who would according to the press releases 'provide guidance and support, be advocates for the young person and, where required, build a long-term relationship with the young person'. They would help ease transition to adulthood and 'build on the new mentoring services now flourishing in the Excellence in Cities programme'. This added to the confusion. Few knew much about 'Excellence in Cities': there had been no evaluation of this limited and essentially urban initiative. What was known was that the DfEE had already set up a 'Youth Support Service Professional Formation Working Group', which had met for the first time in December 1999 with 17 members drawn from the Youth Service, the Careers Service, the Home Office and Department of Health.

The main influence on the group came from Martin Stephenson, seconded from a small voluntary project named 'Include', whose first discussion paper demonstrated just how far away from Careers Service practice was the role of the personal adviser and just how many practical difficulties were to be resolved. Martin Stephenson freely acknowledged that he knew little or nothing about career guidance.

Malcom Wicks, the Minister for Lifelong Learning, who was in a good position to allay fears and lead the debate to a higher level where difficult questions could be addressed, failed to do so. His interview with *Careers Guidance Today* (Wicks 2000) should have been aimed at reassuring career advisers and encouraging their involvement. Instead, it demonstrated his unbridled enthusiasm, and his lack of respect for the reservations honestly held by practitioners. His first reference to them set the tone: 'I understand there are lots of people who are currently in TECs, further education, the Careers Service or the Youth Service who are anxious about what's happening, and understandably they're worried about their positions'. He had missed the point. He went on:

> I hope the personal adviser will say to a young person, 'Okay, we've talked about where you are in terms of your learning journey and options for GCSEs and where you might go for sixth form, but how do you spend your evenings?'
>
> (Wicks 2002: 15)

He had made their point for them.

Wicks' boundless enthusiasm, his uncritical belief in the benefits of change, his lack of knowledge about the young people he was discussing and his disregard for the expertise of those in the existing services did not invite dialogue. He hadn't heard what the Guidance Council, the Institute, the Careers Service National Association and others had been saying. He didn't seem to want to listen.

It was difficult to gauge public reaction to Connexions because there was so little. The February press release was not reported widely. Some newspapers, including *The Times Educational Supplement*, mentioned that young people would be given their mentor's mobile phone number and invited to phone day or night. The *Times* leader on 4 February warned that mentors might be unwelcome in some schools and that parents might wonder about their value. 'A mentor scheme that should not be universally imposed' was the headline. *The Sunday Times* on 1 February suggested that the new scheme would be controversial: 'Some Tory MPs questioned whether £500M would be better spent on teachers and books'.

As the Careers Service absorbed the detail of *Connexions: The Best Start in Life for Every Young Person*, it became apparent that clarification, amendment and improvement would come about largely through the parliamentary process and lobbying, under the leadership of the Guidance Council. The committee stage began in the House of Lords on 10 February. From Baroness Blackstone's replies to questions it soon became clear that, while the Youth Service would be expected to contribute to Connexions, much of its work would continue to go on elsewhere; the Careers Service, however, would be completely absorbed. As Tony Watts pointed out in Guidance Council Bulletin No. 3 (Guidance Council 2000), similar approaches to the Careers Service and the youth service would have avoided many of the concerns which had arisen.

The Youth Service lobby was anxious to see the whole age group included, worried about the prospect of compulsion for young people and averse to any notion of targets for staff. The careers lobby was similarly concerned about what they called universality. Both were equally dubious about the personal adviser role and would have preferred to see youth and careers workers contribute their different skills and expertise to Connexions.

Baroness Blackstone could not have enjoyed the exchanges in the House of Lords. Pressed by Lady David and Baroness Sharp (well briefed by letters from schools, ICG, CSNA and the Guidance Council), she eventually clarified the position:

> I welcome the opportunity to confirm what I perhaps did not make sufficiently clear in Committee. We are not repealing, and do not intend to repeal, any part of the Employment and Training Act 1973. The duties and powers of the Secretary of State to secure Careers Services will, therefore, remain intact.
>
> (Blackstone 2000)

The feeling remained, however, that the government was unsure of its obligations and that their rush to bring in Connexions had led to neglect of career education and guidance. The government's single-minded approach would lead to more long-term problems.

The Careers Service National Association briefing for the House of Commons committee stage stressed the importance of career advice and guidance and the need for universal access. The membership was ready to support the Connexions Strategy but wished to ensure:

- A universal, impartial and independent provision for all young people.
- Sufficient appropriately targeted funding to guarantee a high quality universal service, while affording priority to the most disadvantaged.

- Sound local delivery systems that engaged all relevant partners, which built on best practice and were enabled to evolve so that the government's priorities could be successfully met.

The Institute of Career Guidance briefing was sent to members on 20 March, prior to the Commons Second Reading (earlier than expected on 30 March 2000), urging them to approach MPs locally with very similar messages: that the ICG believed that Connexions could work, but that it should not detract from the universal entitlement to career guidance to all young people; that the professionalism and expertise of the guidance profession should not be undermined, that unrealistic targets could place advisers in a position where advice to return to school or training might not always be in the best interests of the client.

These two statements set the scene for the further stages of legislation which could be expected to continue until the end of July or thereabouts. The Guidance Council policy bulletins continued to provide an invaluable commentary on the process; clear and succinct enough to impress students of public administration in addition to the council's members most directly affected.

Two processes were taking place as they should. MPs, briefed by their constituents, were demanding replies from ministers on how Connexions would actually work and how they could be sure that careers education and guidance would be made available. In preparing replies on behalf of their ministers, civil servants were able to review proposals and make good the detail of the proposed arrangements. These processes continued throughout the second reading in the House of Commons and through the committee stage, the report stage and the third reading, including the passing of amendments between the Commons and the Lords until both were satisfied.

Some progress was made. David Blunkett stated that he intended to expand the role of the Careers Service and to ensure that all young people should receive help. Lord Bach confirmed that personal advisers would be able to refer to careers specialists where necessary. Malcom Wicks confirmed the universal nature of the service. He quoted Richard Titmuss of the London School of Economics, 'if poor people's services are just for poor people, they tend to be poor services' (Wicks 2000a), and proclaimed himself a 'universalist'. Later in the debate Malcolm Wicks announced the appointment of Ann Weinstock of Rathbone Community Industry (on secondment to DfES Millennium Volunteers Project) as head of the Connexions Service National Unit.

The Bill received Royal Assent on 27 July without any major modification. There was a wider acknowledgement of career education and guidance and some guarantee of universality in principle, but the shape of Connexions remained largely unchanged.

Meanwhile, as preparations to launch Connexions continued, so did the level of confusion about exactly how it would work. A quite unexpected complication arose from a DfES circular issued to schools in early May 2000. It seemed to be a belated attempt to mark the partnership expected of schools and local Connexions services, and was written by Stephen Witt of Connexions and Sue Corson of Schools Branch (DfEE 2000a). This circular announced a place for a head teachers' representative on local management committees: a sensible decision. It went on, however, to clarify the position of personal advisers, likening those who were school-based to learning mentors and describing Connexions advisers as assuming responsibilities from the Careers Service. The surprising element, however, was that headteachers were to appoint and manage the personal advisers working in their schools. This raised difficult issues of impartiality, accountability and division of the Connexions budget.

It was also at odds with another policy paper released in May, *The Connexions Service: Prospectus and Specification* (DfEE 2000), which detailed partnership arrangements for local structures and delivery and asked for submission of outline proposals by local partnerships before 9 June. It suggested that Connexions partnerships would lead on determining how personal advisers would operate in schools. The impression given was that branches of DfEE were beginning to spot the weaknesses and omissions from their earlier Connexions drafts and that deals were being done between officials based at Great Smith Street, the London headquarters of the Schools Division, and Moorfoot, the Sheffield office of the Careers Service National Unit. The prospectus and specification also included reference to best value and sub-contracting, a belated acknowledgement that Careers Service companies might continue to play a role in some localities.

While some modifications in the Connexions strategy were taking place, Wales and Scotland were working their way towards independent and different alternatives. The National Assembly for Wales decided at the end of 1999 to set up an expert group to consider what would best meet the interests of young people in Wales (Welsh National Assembly 2000). This group included a youth officer and a chief executive of a careers company. The First Secretary made it clear that consultation with the Welsh Local Government Association would be extensive. He had already received agreement from the UK cabinet to insert specific clauses in the Learning and Skills Bill. Careers Wales was to be the eventual outcome.

Scotland's solution was to emerge from the Beattie Committee, which reported in May 2000. Henry McLeish had set up the committee 18 months previously under the chairmanship of Robert Beattie, IBM's Community Investment Co-ordinator. Significantly, careers professionals were also involved in Scotland, as in Wales. Julie Ann Jamieson was seconded from Fife Careers Service to support the work of the committee. The Beattie Committee considered inclusiveness, which involved:

- Valuing the person as a whole.
- Recognising a spectrum of needs and capabilities.
- Providing a stream of learning opportunities.

It recognised the need for more co-ordination of services and better information about individuals and services, and recommended the creation of a 'key worker' who would not replace existing services but would act as first contact where necessary. Amongst the specific recommendations was support for the 'crucial role played by the Careers Service in the transition process'. The Scottish Executive immediately put in place a National Action Group to provide a national focus. Careers Scotland was to be the outcome.

In June the government released yet another internal Connexions document, *The Connexions Service: Framework for Personal Advisers* (DfEE 2000a). This was a consultation document requiring a response in the form of a questionnaire by 27 July but consisted largely of information about the proposed 'new profession'.

In July Ann Weinstock took up her appointment as Head of the National Unit. As a member of the government's Skills Task Force, she was already on secondment to the Department as Director of 'Millennium Volunteers'. Mrs Weinstock had previously been head of Rathbone CI and a member of Manchester Training and Enterprise Council. Her salary was within a minimum range of £75,000 to £95,000, reviewed annually.

On 6 July Malcolm Wicks addressed the annual conference of the National Association of Careers and Guidance Teachers. Seeking to allay their fears about the partial withdrawal of careers advisers from schools, he emphasised universal access to careers education and guidance. He was unspecific, however, following his familiar line on ICT, call centres, mobile phones and 'Connexions Direct', on the need to consult young people, and the prospects for a 'Youth Parliament'.

On 27 July the Learning and Skills Bill received final assent. On 23 October David Blunkett announced that the 16 pilot areas would receive funding in the next financial year and that the Connexions budget would amount to £420 million by the end of 2002/3 – an increase of £177 million over the existing budget of the Careers Service. The 16 Connexions Partnerships were confirmed as: Milton Keynes, Oxfordshire and Buckinghamshire; London

North; London South; West of England; Cornwall and Devon; the Black Country; Coventry and Warwickshire; Shropshire, Telford and Wrekin; Lincolnshire and Rutland; South Yorkshire; Humberside; Cheshire and Warrington; Cumbria; Suffolk, due to start in July; Greater Merseyside; and Tyne and Wear in September.

But, while the scene was set and preparations well advanced, the basic problems around Connexions remained unsolved. In particular the whole concept of the personal adviser remained intractable. All the work of the Professional Formation Group, the mapping of the competencies and consultation processes could not solve that problem.

At the ICG annual conference Tom Wylie, Head of the National Youth Agency, had repeated and clarified the doubts expressed by the Youth Service throughout the short history of Connexions. He pointed out (Wylie 2000) that the proposed 'new professional' was arguably the only big idea in Connexions. But while he saw a case for a key worker, he personally would not approach the issue in this way. He would redefine the existing professions: careers officers, youth workers and educational welfare officers. His belief was that professionals in a variety of roles should be trained to work alongside other agencies.

Ken Roberts joined the debate, pointing out that career guidance would be at the heart of Connexions and that whatever problems beset young people, they almost always had educational and job implications. 'Careers guidance officers were the people who possessed the generic skills that Connexions required' (Roberts 2000).

Ann Weinstock (Weinstock 2001), her speech read for her by civil servant Steve Geary as she was in hospital, confirmed that careers education and guidance would be the cornerstone of Connexions. She confessed, however, that while more had to be done to explain the proposals, something more than presentation was involved. She apologised for spreading alarm and despondency.

When the Connexions Planning Guidance came out in October, it modified the proposal that all young people should have a personal adviser, and talked instead of all having access to guidance, including impartial guidance on career choices for those for whom it was needed. Once again the situation was clouded by references to the Connexions website and Connexions Direct, but it seemed that specialist career advisers would remain.

An update to the Planning Guidance later drew distinctions between kinds of 'Connexions advisers': 'Connexions personal advisers' and 'specialist advisers'. Connexions advisers were to include 'careers worker'; specialist advisers were to include those who would deal with specialised aspects of learning and careers – for example, special needs.

It seemed that policy was eventually being refined. The operation of Connexions was taking shape, but there was still some way to go. Ann Weinstock, returning to work from illness in time to give the annual lecture at the Centre for Guidance Studies in November, demonstrated the remaining ambiguities. Even her title, 'Connexions and Youth Policy: A Brighter Future', exemplified confusion (Weinstock 2001). She sought to reassure, apologising as she had to the ICG for 'pissing people off', and confessing that operational problems were causing difficulty. But her approach, injudicious language, random examples and overuse of personal anecdote, obscured any wider vision. She appeared to make clear, however, that she had understood the need for impartial career guidance and the continuing need for careers specialists.

Weinstock's broad interests in youth policy, information technology, community involvement and a new approach to the delivery of services reflect the preoccupations of the government as a whole. The danger of ever wider divergence in the name of diversity left Careers Services without a clear policy or operational framework. Tony Watts' warnings of fundamental design flaws in the Connexions strategy (Watts 2001) rang true.

The first twelve Connexions partnerships began work in April 2001 and were joined by three more in September 2001. The intention was that all 47 partnerships, covering the whole country, would be up and running in 2003. The Learning and Skills Act required that the areas to be covered would be coterminous with those of local Learning and Skills Councils.

The Careers Service company structure provided a firm basis for local partnerships. Local authorities made arrangements for the appointment of chief executives in some areas, Careers Service company boards in others. Advertisements appeared in social service supplements (of the *Guardian*, for example), rather than in the educational press where Careers Service appointments had previously been advertised. Advertisements followed a fixed format, with salaries apparently calculated on a formula. Despite strong pressure from the centre, one or two areas refused to advertise, appointing their existing Careers Service chief executives directly. In many areas the existing Careers Service chief executive was the successful candidate after advertisement and selection processes had been completed.

Connexions Partnerships were responsible for making the appointments. These Partnerships included representatives of local authorities, local health authorities, the youth service, voluntary organisations, the local Learning and Skills Council, schools, the probation service, police and youth offending teams. Forty-four Partnerships were operating by the end of 2002. The intention was to complete coverage by approving schemes for the three remaining areas by the end of 2003.

As Connexions Partnerships became responsible for operating the new service two ways of doing so emerged. Many adopted the 'transmutation' approach. The Careers Service company in this case was 'transmuted' into the Connexions Partnership and became the Connexions provider. In other areas Careers Service companies continued to provide the service on the basis of contracts issued by Connexions partnerships established as companies limited by guarantee. While 'transmuted' services are the rule, 'contracted' services usually operate in densely populated areas such as the Midlands and the south-east, where the large Career Development Group remains the main provider.

An interesting development began to take shape towards the end of 2002 when representatives of the 'contracted' services met to plan 'Careers England', an association of Careers Service companies dedicated to providing high quality career guidance to clients of all ages. Their intention was to launch their new association in February 2003.

It is difficult to see just how this association will figure in the plans of the Connexions Service National Unit. Attention there is still fixed on the generalist role of the personal adviser which Tom Wylie, head of the National Youth Agency, had pointed out, was arguably the only big idea in Connexions. The *Connexions Business Planning Guidance 2003–2004* described how personal advisers (of whom 2,500 have now received in-service training) are 'taking responsibility for helping young people with complex needs, arranging help from more specialist services where necessary, making sure that people are no longer passed on from one agency to another' (CSNU 2002: 7). They often pass clients from one personal adviser to another, however. In most Connexions areas the universal personal adviser is seen as a careers adviser who will also deal with benefits, housing and leisure issues. But it is by no means certain that the Connexions Service National Unit is satisfied with this. A more general role is envisaged: 'brokering access' to others seems to be an important element, as does 'removing obstacles' and being 'the lead professional'.

This difficulty in defining the work of the personal adviser featured in the first report of OFSTED, *Connexions Partnerships: the first year 2001–2002*, issued in October 2002 (OFSTED had been made the body responsible for inspection by the Learning and Skills Act). The report pointed out that, while most young people responded positively to the work of the personal adviser, 'There is a lack of clarity about the role and deployment across many partnership areas and within schools' (OFSTED 2002). OFSTED appeared to be broadly equating the personal adviser with the careers adviser, pointing out that 'Where Connexions practice is developing well, the careers professional in the role of careers adviser provides a holistic approach to the support of young people's learning and complements the pastoral and academic goals of the school or college'.

While the inspectors were critical of the variable quality of career guidance for young people already on work-based training and found that information on work-based training opportunities in many schools was poor, they were positive about the welcome for personal advisers in schools:

> The first experience in many schools of the Connexions Service was the development of the careers adviser role into the personal adviser. Most schools welcome this because they perceive the additional time involved as going some way to restoring their allocation of careers guidance expertise which had been lost over previous years.
>
> (OFSTED 2002)

While the inspectors did not say so, the previous years referred to were those since 1997, the time of 'refocusing'.

But the ambivalence of the Connexions Service National Unit towards career guidance persists. Their *Business Planning Guidance 2003–4* is difficult to interpret but where it is being positive it says that: 'the Connexions Service should make available to all young people initial advice on career and learning options but not in depth career guidance' (CSNU 2002: 12). It makes what it calls a clear statement of what the Connexions Service is not: 'It is not the provision solely for the majority (as distinct from the targeted or intensive services). Nor is it the delivery solely of careers information, advice and guidance' (CSNU 2000: 12).

Perhaps this is simply a question of writing style: too many words, some of them in the wrong order. But the Unit's vision for 2006 adds to the confusion. It is clear about Connexions listening to young people and being a 'learning organisation'. It is clear about the Youth Service, which will be 'vibrant and high quality in each area'. It makes only one reference to career guidance, which will be made available to: 'those who need it when they need it as part of a broader package' (CSNU 2002: 12).

The impression given is that the majority may not need career guidance at all and those who do might be referred to specialists. Until the National Unit sorts out the ambiguity of the personal adviser's role and its own ambivalence towards career guidance, there must be some concern within DfES about whether the statutory responsibility to provide a Careers Service is being met in England. If personal advisers from Connexions are not to provide career guidance, then who is?

All the remaining careers companies and most Connexions Partnerships have continued their work with adults through Information, Advice and Guidance (IAG) partnerships, many taking the lead role. IAGs are quite separate organisations using separate staff. They originate from the 1999 White

Paper 'Learning to Succeed', which recognised the need to improve services to adults. Additional resources followed, distributed through partnerships of local providers. The government transferred responsibility for funding and planning to the Learning and Skills Council in April 2001.

Close working relationships between Connexions and IAG have not yet been developed, but Geoff Ford, a NICEC Fellow, has put forward some interesting proposals in *The Connexions Strategy and All-age Guidance*, an occasional paper published by the Centre for Guidance Studies (Ford 2002). Ford argues that Connexions principles can apply equally to adults and young people. He considers the possibility of introducing 'Guidance Action Zones' to provide a framework for collaboration between IAG and Connexions, and comments on the opportunities for coherence provided by comparing provision in different parts of the United Kingdom.

Ford's work with the Third Age Employment Network and the Challenging Age Research Project (due to be published in 2003) seems likely to draw further conclusions about ways in which the needs of adults can be met.

Meanwhile, the independent solutions adopted by Wales and Scotland have continued to develop. Careers Wales and Careers Scotland embody the same belief in a single service providing career guidance for people of all ages but each has adopted its own approach.

Careers Wales was formed in April 2001 with the lifelong learning agenda very much in mind. The National Assembly's Policy Unit report *Extending Entitlement: supporting young people in Wales* recommended that the new service would work best by improving support at National Assembly level for the existing services and operating through the seven careers companies already covering the whole of the country. Careers Wales provides 70 careers centres operated by seven companies. They work under the common brand of 'Careers Wales' and are therefore more easily recognisable than before. Their remit is wider, carrying responsibility for encouraging employers' links with schools and colleges and for helping community organisations encourage adults back to learning.

Careers Wales is a universal service for young people, which pays particular attention to those in danger of dropping out, providing specialist support for those with special needs and taking care in the placing of unemployed young people. It provides free advice and information for adults calling at careers centres and free guidance for unemployed adults and those seeking to improve their employment prospects. Employers receive a free recruitment service when recruiting young people, and advice on training questions and links with education.

Careers Scotland, the eventual outcome of the Beattie Committee's report and the Scottish Executive's National Action Group, was launched in March

2002. Like Careers Wales, it is an all-age guidance service with a national brand easily recognisable to young people and adults throughout the country.

Formed by merging the pre-existing careers companies with adult guidance networks and education business partnerships, Careers Scotland is a private enterprise, directly funded by the Scottish Executive and operated through Scottish Enterprise and Highland and Islands Enterprise. It falls within the Department of the Minister for Enterprise, Transport and Lifelong Learning.

The emphasis on the economic and enterprise elements of career guidance pervades Careers Scotland. Social exclusion is approached from this perspective: vulnerable young people are seen as needing good training and employment opportunities. Adults, employed or unemployed, are also helped with advice on choosing careers and assistance in finding opportunities that will suit them.

Both Wales and Scotland have arrived at similar Careers Services in different ways. Scotland has emphasised the 'economic' elements, Wales the 'educational' elements. Both differ fundamentally from the 'social' approach and the restrictions applied in England.

The situation in Northern Ireland is different again but largely because decisions about the structure of Careers Services there have been delayed. The Institute of Career Guidance briefing paper, *Career Guidance in Northern Ireland: A Service in Transition* (Hopkins 2002), issued in July 2002, pointed out that 'while the structure of the Careers Service in Northern Ireland remains as it was, its aims and priorities have been reshaped to meet the agenda set by the Northern Ireland Executive'.

Careers officers in Northern Ireland are civil servants employed by the Department of Employment and Learning, operating from Jobcentres. In principle the service is not restricted to young people; in practice careers officers work largely in schools and colleges, supporting careers education and interviewing individuals. An Educational Guidance Service for Adults (an independent voluntary body) receives direct government funding to provide guidance for those working to extend or access their own learning.

The Northern Ireland Assembly is aware of the need to strengthen career guidance. The opening of a training course leading to the qualification in career guidance at the University of Ulster in 2002 suggests that the need for careers advisers to staff an expanding service is also understood. Northern Ireland needs time. It has the basis of an all-age guidance service if it chooses to build upon it. It seems reasonable to speculate that something on the lines of Careers Wales or Careers Scotland might be the eventual outcome.

It might be argued that the variety of provision which has emerged and is developing in different parts of the UK demonstrates the essence of devolution; that each country has adapted the system likely to suit it best. It is difficult to imagine, however, that every approach is equally effective in meeting the needs of individuals, the education system, the economy and society in general. What diversity provides is the opportunity for comparison. Careful research into the ways in which career guidance is made available in different parts of the United Kingdom in 2002 could provide a firm basis for the next stage in the evaluation of Careers Services, for it seems unlikely that the present pattern will remain unchanged for very long.

Chapter 7

Some conclusions

The introduction set out the dual aim of this book: to chronicle a century of the service created to help young people choose a pathway through life, and to draw conclusions which might help to provide a basis for future policy. The idea is well expressed by Lord Melchett's 1911 review of reform in the previous century: 'It looked as though each generation in turn had gathered force to carry forward the movement which their predecessors had begun' (NAJEWO 1928). The underlying philosophy is contained in the well-known quotation from Santayana in 1905: 'Those who cannot remember the past are condemned to repeat it.' This concluding chapter will examine the efforts of succeeding generations of policy-makers, administrators and practitioners to find the best way of delivering career guidance, draw conclusions, consider how the lessons learned might be useful to those contemplating changes in the future, and then examine some of the changes already taking place at the end of 2002.

The three characteristics which had already emerged by 1948 have proved remarkably persistent throughout the century. They are:

- An uncertain administrative framework.
- A body of dedicated professionals able to exert influence individually and collectively (often punching above their weight).
- Increasing awareness of the educational, social and economic value of career guidance as the century has progressed.

To these three, two more observations may be added:

- The balance between the three elements of educational, social and economic policy in career guidance services may change but all three need to be present to some extent.
- The concept of the dedicated professional emerged from the belief founded on experience, that objective, impartial career guidance is best provided

by trained specialists independent of educational institutions and employer interests.

These broad characteristics are not difficult to discern. Identifying more specific lessons from a complex history is more difficult.

From the early days of the Juvenile Employment and Welfare Service through the Youth Employment Service, the Careers Service and the service provided by careers companies, a number of lessons emerge and are presented below in more or less chronological order:

- Choosing a career is essentially an educational process. Those who provide help should be close to schools and colleges and adopt a broadly educational approach to their work.
- Responsibility for providing a service should be clear and unambiguous nationally and locally. Split responsibility creates wasteful dispute and dissension.
- Youth defies close definition in terms of career choice. Artificially imposed age limits cannot be successfully applied.
- Career advisers require specific training in the theory and practice of their work.
- Professional identity provides motivation to improve practice and play a part in the development of sound policy.
- A successful career guidance service requires a strong central voice within the Department responsible for putting policy into practice.
- Continuing involvement of practitioners with policy-making, including direct contact with politicians of all parties, is likely to improve the quality of policy and its application.
- Practitioners must be able to understand, apply and refine the theory of careers education and guidance, to learn from and in turn influence psychologists, sociologists and labour economists.
- Careers education is most likely to be successful if delivered by skilled, experienced teachers working in partnership with career advisers.
- Career advisers need a wide knowledge of jobs and those likely to succeed in them if they are to meet the expectations of young people, parents and other adults.
- The economic value of career guidance and the importance of close contact with the needs of employers can be underestimated by practitioners and managers alike.
- Working with both young people and adults benefits clients, practitioners and the service itself.
- The use of private companies to provide a career guidance service must

allow scope for innovation and professional exploration. Ways must be found to disseminate information and share experience between companies.

- A national service must be easily recognisable whoever provides it locally. Company names and logos can confuse.
- Change is expensive. Money spent on reforming a service may not provide value for money if the new arrangements are not allowed to mature. Frequent change is wasteful of human and financial resources.

It would be convenient to believe that this list of lessons learned from history could be arranged in a sort of matrix against which future proposals for change in career guidance services could be measured. This list provides a number of indicators which should be considered but that is all. It is necessary to take account of wider contemporary change before trying to make judgements about the effectiveness of the way present policy is being applied or future policy might be developed.

For example, it could be argued that the most successful periods in the history of career guidance have been those when trust between politicians, civil servants and practitioners has been strongest. The post-war period of the Youth Employment Service provides a good example as does the mid 1970s, the early days of the Careers Service. The compromise between education and employment interests then produced a sound administrative base which at that time was arguably as good as any in the world. Central responsibility vested in the Employment Department, local responsibility resting with local education authorities, careers advisers working closely with schools but independent of them, produced a partnership which was vital and dynamic and rested upon mutual trust.

An even better example is the more recent experiment with careers companies, conceived and originally operated on the basis of trust. Once career advisers had accepted the intention behind the legislation they were ready to move into a period of innovation and expansion which had the potential to influence education and the labour market to the full extent envisaged by the civil servants who had conceived the new arrangements. Ironically it was the Department of Education and Employment which lost faith in its own judgement and imposed an audit regime so severe that it suppressed initiative and skewed policy. The contract between the Department and the companies should have been sufficient. Excessive audit and target setting seemed to indicate lack of trust in provider and practitioner alike.

The introduction of focusing, or 'refocusing', was carried out after the general election without the careful consultation with companies and practitioners which might have improved its effectiveness by refining the policy objective and demonstrating trust. Subsequently the rapid development of the

Connexions strategy in England continued with only minimal contact between political advisers and civil servants on one hand and on the other the companies and practitioners who would be relied upon to put the strategy into operation. This too seemed to indicate a lack of trust, which applied not only to the Careers Service but to public services in general. In her Reith Lecture in April 2002, Onora O'Neill, philosopher and Principal of Newnham College, Cambridge, examined the whole topic of trust in the public services and those who work in them. She questioned the audit culture and its application to the public sector, suggesting that performance indicators often measure that which is easy to measure, 'quality' becomes conformity, more information does not result in more trust. Measurement diverts resources from service. It can undermine judgement and autonomy.

O'Neill stated that intelligent accountability is more about good governance and less about total control. Control needs to be exercised by professionals, to be normative rather than arithmetical, based on question and answer. She concluded that most public servants have a central ethical standard. Making them run races will not help. Better to use an inspection system which allows conversation between peers. She argued that people give informed consent on the basis of trust throughout their daily lives. We assess, but rely on others. We place trust in those giving counsel and rely on the integrity of the adviser.

Naturally, Onora O'Neill's main concerns centred upon health and education and the professions at work within them: she did not have the Careers Service in mind. But Sir Christopher Ball, when Chairman of the Guidance Council, prophesied that guidance would take its place alongside teaching, law and medicine as one of the great professions of the twenty-first century. Whether or not Christopher Ball's vision is supportable is a debate in itself but the growth of public interest in career guidance, notable throughout 100 years of development in the UK, has an international dimension which is having its effect upon careers advisers in Britain. International symposia on connecting career development and public policy, held in 1999 and 2001, have done much to focus their attention on their own professional training and effect on public policy-making.

Lynne Bezanson, Executive Director of the Canadian Career Development Foundation, herself a careers counsellor, organised these symposia and addressed the ICG Conference on Policy and Practice in September 2002 (Bezanson 2001). Her theme was that Careers Services become more and more important as global, economic and technological change require people to manage transitions effectively. Career advisers have limited access to those who make the policy into which their clients must fit. But they hold information based on these clients' experiences which could be invaluable to the formation of sound policy if made immediately available to policy-makers, driven as they are by data and evidence required to justify expenditure. The challenge is to find indicators which not only confirm improvements to placing on schemes, reducing unemployment and meeting targets, but to find acceptable indicators of the value of career adaptability (and thereby demonstrate the effectiveness of the adviser). Bezanson was also keen to find ways of increasing public demand for the benefits of career guidance.

This approach has direct and urgent messages for career advisers in the UK, whatever their work setting. A dialogue with politicians, civil servants and opinion formers, based on knowledge of clients and their needs, could do much to allay distrust. If it were to be based on mutually acceptable success criteria and on research, it could itself provide the basis of future policy change. If it were to become continuous, it could insure policy-makers against expensive mistakes and practitioners against having to fight rearguard actions in order to modify mistaken policies.

This public policy theme also echoes from another international development. In 2001 the OECD recruited Tony Watts, retiring from his position as NICEC Director, to take part in its first survey of career guidance relating to lifelong learning. Fourteen countries took part. The report had not been written by the end of 2002 but Watts, speaking to the ICG Conference in September, was able to indicate some of the main conclusions (Watts 2002). It had emerged from fieldwork that all the countries taking part were about to re-examine their career guidance systems in the light of lifelong learning policy. All were concerned that existing systems were concentrated on the unemployed and on young people. The need now is to provide a service for those who are outside the labour market or seeking to develop a career and for career guidance which goes beyond the simple provision of career information. The report seems likely to have particular relevance for Careers Services in England when it is presented in the Spring of 2003.

Closer to home is another international development likely to benefit the development of career guidance services in the UK. The 'Home Internationals' conferences held in Belfast in 1999 and 2001 provided opportunities for representatives of services in England, Northern Ireland, the Republic of Ireland, Scotland and Wales to compare their experiences. The 2001 session included 36 representatives who discussed co-operative action on a range of topics including the selection, training and retention of career guidance practitioners. Another conference is planned for 2003 (CRAC/NICEC 2001).

International issues such as globalisation, concern about skill shortages, the composition of the workforce as older workers remain economically active and the number of young recruits declines, seem likely to focus attention on the economic value of career guidance to adults and young people alike.

The education system too will find itself in need of a more effective Careers Service.

The government's Green Paper '14–19 Extending Opportunities, Raising Standards' has reopened the debate about the role of teachers involved in careers education and their relationship to the impartial careers advisers who must work closely with them if objective guidance is to be brought to bear on the choices pupils will make at the age of 14. The 'Connexions strategy' is less talked about now. The Connexions service remains ready, perhaps, to alter course in the light of experience and a new steer from the government.

There are wider indications that social policy-making in the United Kingdom is entering a new phase. Despite the Prime Minister's assertion to the TUC's annual conference in 2002 that ' the radical decision is usually the right one', the strength of 'the project' which accompanied the new Labour Government in 1997 seems to be waning. Disillusionment with generic social work, highlighted by a succession of tragic cases of child abuse, may well contribute to the break-up of social service departments and recognition of the contribution which can be made by specialists such as children's officers. Simply bringing workers under one administrative umbrella does not ensure co-operation or guarantee efficiency.

It is predictable too that the general move to central control, so strong in the first four years of the Labour Government, will become less fashionable. Regionalism has been slow to materialise in the wake of devolution but will be realised in time. 'Localism' will replace centralism, 'command structures' may be overtaken by 'local diversity'. Freedom from central control for success-ful hospitals and local authorities may be the first sign. The proposed regional governments charged with economic development, working with Learning and Skills Councils and local education authorities in England, might well prefer Careers Services on the lines of Scotland and Wales to a 'one size fits all' Connexions service. The likelihood of a new regional government in the North East will provide an interesting test-bed.

Social policy and social administration both seem ready for further review as the government realises how much further it has to go to reach its wider objectives. Onora O'Neill's view of the centrality of trust in the public services and Lynne Bezanson's approach to dialogue between policy-makers and professionals may well become more influential as a result.

Challenging the existing social class structure provides intriguing possi-bilities for further change. The intention to encourage up to 50 per cent of young people from a wider social background to enter higher education demonstrates the government's awareness of this. Higher education may be a useful place to start but the effects of social class are more fundamental than has been generally realised: class is one determinant of length of life. While the average life expectancy has increased dramatically since 1902, there are significant differences amongst occupational groups. In 1972, men in low paid jobs could expect to die aged 66.5, men in professional jobs could expect to live for a further 5.5 years. By 1999, low paid men could expect to die aged 71 and professional men to live for a further 7.4 years; the gap is increasing (Nicholson 2002). In *Class in Modern Britain* (Roberts 2001), Ken Roberts points out that occupation remains the basis of class and that social mobility has not increased to the extent expected. He describes 'the absence of major variations between modern societies and over time within those societies' as one of the most startling discoveries in the whole of sociology. He goes on to say that this finding, one of sociology's major findings, has been ignored by virtually all social policy-makers.

This brief excursion into vital statistics and sociological theory is not a preliminary to making exaggerated claims for the value of career guidance. Drastic changes in the way work is made available, organised and rewarded would be necessary to bring about major improvement. But some of those whose working lives are unsatisfactory and whose contribution to the economy and society is less than it could be, are simply in the wrong jobs. Career advisers, whose expertise depends largely on their knowledge of jobs and those who succeed in them, should have something to say about that.

The lesson to be learned from 100 years of career guidance is that careers is a very political business. The choices people make about the work they do goes some way to deciding how and for how long they live their lives. The way governments choose to help individuals make choices wisely affects society, the economy and the education system which can fail if this essential component, impartial career guidance, is not readily available to all. Writing about socio-political ideologies in guidance in 1996, Tony Watts put it even more forcefully:

> Careers education and guidance is a profoundly political process. It operates at the interface between the individual and society, between self and opportunity, between aspiration and realism. It facilitates the allocation of life chances. Within a society in which life chances are unequally distributed, it faces the issue of whether it serves to reinforce such inequalities or reduce them.
>
> (Watts 1996: 351)

It is useful at this point to see how these developments and potential changes might fit with the three persistent characteristics of career guidance services for young people in the United Kingdom. To reiterate they are:

- An uncertain administrative framework.
- A body of dedicated practitioners able to exert influence individually or collectively.
- Increasing awareness of the educational, social and economic value of career guidance.

Take the last one first. International interest, investment in Connexions and IAG, Careers Wales and Careers Scotland and the recent 14–19 White Paper 'Opportunity and Excellence' all provide evidence that the value of career guidance continues to provide debate for policy-makers and practitioners and suggests that interest probably continues to increase.

The uncertainty of the administrative framework seems as evident at the end of 2002 as it was in 1948. It is difficult to believe that the present structure, introduced so hastily in England before the changes of only five years previously had become established, will remain as it is. Perhaps the lesson to be drawn from this is wider and more fundamental than the nature of the present framework. Perhaps it demonstrates that governments, carried away with their enthusiasm to provide career guidance in their own ways, cannot be trusted to take account of history and experience when devising administrative structures capable of delivering their policies. They need help. To use the present government's favourite phrase: they must work in partnership.

This brings the remaining persistent characteristic into play; the body of dedicated practitioners able to exert influence individually and collectively. In fact they have done more than this. At the beginning of the 1970s and in the early 1980s, to take two examples, practitioners were able to punch above their weight, convincing governments that their strongly held views represented the needs of their clients, their colleagues (especially teachers) and themselves. The question to be answered is how far they can continue to exert influence in the aftermath of two contrasting but fundamental reorganisations of their work within one decade, and in anticipation of continuing change.

There is no shortage of expertise in influencing policy. Many of the senior members and officers of the Institute of Career Guidance, for example, have recent experience of modifying and improving government proposals. In doing so they have helped successive governments avoid the consequences of their more extreme proposals. Their difficulty has been that the increasing control exercised by central government has left them reacting rather than contributing to policy; often fighting what looks like a rearguard action. Career advisers working in Connexions are similarly experienced and well-placed, especially those who are now chief executives. The Careers Service National Association was wound up in October 2002 but a successor body, perhaps a national association of Connexions Partnerships, is likely to be formed in 2003.

The Institute has strengthened its position overall, however, by concentrating on its professional standing and improving the services it offers to members. An important influence in this process has been Terry Collins, the Chair of the Institute's Ethics and Standards Committee. He has argued over three decades for publicly measurable professional standards, for a widening of the profession well beyond the Careers Service and for career guidance practitioners (he would prefer the term 'vocational guidance') to see themselves as more independent of the organisations within which they work. Collins is just one of a number of influential individuals who have contributed to the debate on professionalism in career guidance but his ideas are indicative of the direction the Institute and the profession as a whole are beginning to take.

A number of recent changes demonstrate the progress which has been made:

- There is a greater awareness of the international dimension of career guidance. The 'Home Internationals' and International Symposia on Career Development and Public Policy have contributed to this. Interest in the International Association for Educational and Vocational Guidance has also quickened with a number of prominent British career advisers playing an active part.
- The Institute's decision to petition for a Royal Charter also demonstrates confidence. The idea is not new, it dates back to 1969, but there is a new realism, an understanding of how difficult it will be for a body with less than 5,000 members to meet the Privy Council's criteria.
- The formation of the Federation of Professional Associations in Guidance with a seat on the Guidance Council is a clear acknowledgement of a wide professional base.
- The Institute's commendable Register of Practitioners is likely to interest all the professional associations in guidance. More than a simple list of members, it comprises a register of those who are qualified to practise and have undertaken to continue their professional development in order to continue to serve clients directly. They work to a specified code of practice and offer a complaints procedure to dissatisfied clients (Collins 2001).
- The Institute made an important step in 1999 when it assumed responsibility for the qualifying examinations, the Qualification in Career Guidance and the Diploma in Career Guidance. Training emerged as a major concern from the international symposia and the Home Internationals.
- A further sign of professional confidence and awareness of continuing change lies in the Institute's decision in February 2002 to support the implementation of an all-age guidance service for England. Career advisers should be able to work with young people and adults to their mutual

advantage. Young people especially are likely to benefit from the expertise of career advisers experienced in helping older workers deal with the problems which arise in mid-career.

- There is increased interest in research and evidence-based practice. Research centres at, for example, the universities of Derby, Nottingham Trent, Strathclyde and Warwick are led by prominent members of the career guidance profession.
- Masters degrees are now available in many of the 16 universities which run Qualifications in Career Guidance courses and post-graduate diplomas' in career guidance.

Taken as a whole these developments provide a firm foundation from which a body of dedicated professionals can continue to exert influence. The base should widen as more practitioners grow to understand the value of co-operative action. Influence should increase proportionately to the extent of direct and consistent contact with politicians of all parties. The lesson of the need for dialogue with representatives of public opinion, well illustrated by international symposia, should be applied.

It is from this position that practitioners can best play their part, concentrating on their function rather than the environment in which it is performed; looking objectively at the services in which they work by applying Alec Rodger's criteria from 1951, half-way through this history. Rodger's three criteria: how far is a service politically defensible, technically sound and administratively convenient, hold good in 2002.

Time spent on pondering the best ways to make career guidance readily available to people is not wasted. In his Reith Lecture in December 2002, Rowan Williams, the new Archbishop of Canterbury, considered the relationship between the authority of the state and its relations with individuals. He described the emergence of a 'market state' applying consumerism to the business of government, responding rapidly to pressure. Williams' concern was with the effects of this rapid reaction on fundamental questions like the environment and education. He argued that people need involvement in the future as well as the present if they are to make sense of their lives: to feel themselves part of 'a greater story'. The need is to see one's own life in terms of cumulative experience, of many others moving in similar patterns.

At the end of 100 years of history it is not unduly pretentious to point out that career guidance is a small part of that greater story. By providing time and opportunity for individuals to reflect on their pathways through life it contributes to the lifelong process of education and conscious assimilation to society.

What individuals need from their career advisers is wisdom, perception and discretion, the sound application of experience and knowledge to their own particular situation, and tolerance of the ambiguity of the human condition when making decisions.

One hundred years of history illustrates some progress in this direction. The best career guidance services for the future will be those which place fewest barriers between adviser and client.

Addendum

During the House of Commons debate on 14–19 Education on 14 February 2003, Graham Brady MP, the Conservative Schools spokesman, expressed concern that insufficient priority would be attached to guidance in the implementation of the government's proposals. He quoted the Guidance Council's call for a universal service to be delivered by personal advisers with career guidance skills and drew attention to the absence of a statutory framework for careers education and guidance which would guarantee entitlement to one-to-one support.

Ivan Lewis MP, the Minister concerned, referred to the need to put in place a number of building blocks, the first being the quality of advice, information and guidance. He later stressed that the service must be independent and of high quality. It must be universal in the sense that all must have access to it but must recognise that some need more support than others. He went on to say that he would soon be issuing guidance on the provision of career guidance from the age of eleven (he probably meant to say 'careers education').

Whilst not a ringing endorsement of a general need for help in making career choices, this was nevertheless an acknowledgement that the debate continues about the position in England.

The principle of providing impartial career guidance was reiterated in March when *Careers Education and Guidance in England: A National Framework 11–19* was issued by the Department for Education and Skills. This document presents a national non-statutory framework for careers education and guidance but places responsibility for co-ordinating careers work firmly with schools and colleges (DfES 2003).

The Connexions Service is specifically mentioned as aiming to support every young person by ensuring access to advice, information and guidance. Connexions Partnerships are expected to support the delivery of careers education through curriculum developments and teacher training. Careers education programmes should include information on the role of Connexions in 'learning, work, health, housing, finance and the law, and access to the service at a level appropriate to their individual need' (DfES 2003).

Connexions is also mentioned under 'Securing coherent guidance provision'. Here, the various different sources of specialist guidance are listed, with a proposal that a school should set up a 'guidance forum'. Connexions is defined as including the help that Careers Services previously provided but more extensive, including finance, health, welfare and 'the need for intensive help and multi-agency support' (DfES 2003).

Despite the careful language the ambiguous position of the Department on the Connexions Service as a Careers Service cannot be avoided. The impression given is that all young people have easy access to impartial career advice and guidance, as they did under the Careers Service. In reality, schools are being asked to act as gatekeepers and the service to which they may refer young people is described more as a general youth support service than a Careers Service. The Department also seems confused about careers information, advice and guidance. It is understandable, perhaps, that they should be seen as a whole but there is an absence of definition and a lack of information about how and where guidance and advice on careers can be found by the majority of young people.

This confusion is becoming apparent in the way Connexions is perceived in the wider educational community. Apart from occasional questions of the confidentiality of information held on individual young people, Connexions has received very little media attention. In July 2003, however, two newspapers carried articles on careers advice for young people in England. Both were based on discussions held at the Association of Colleges annual conference. The *Financial Times* reported that the new 'careers and advice service' had abandoned middle-class children, leaving schools to advise their own pupils, with a consequent emphasis on remaining in sixth forms. *The Independent* on 3 July took a similar line, reporting a college principal's statement that drop-out from higher education was mainly due to inappropriate career choice. The complexity of choices available means that many young people require impartial advice.

The lack of clarity about the availability of career guidance for young people in England also emerged strongly from the OECD's *Review of Career Guidance Policies*, published in April 2003. *The United Kingdom Country Note*, written by Richard Sweet of OECD's Secretariat, points out that the UK now has many of the features of a country with a federal system of government. He refers to the growing divergence between the ways in which careers guidance is provided since the introduction of Connexions (OECD 2003).

Amongst the policy issues identified for the UK government, the report includes the need to monitor careers education and guidance in schools in the light of continuing concern that career guidance in schools may be reduced. It identifies the skills, qualifications and competence of Connexions staff as particularly important and refers to the lack of clarity of nomenclature of career guidance practitioners and to shortcomings in the diploma for personal advisers.

The report describes Careers Wales as a national all-age career guidance service with a common brand name, reflecting the policy of career guidance at the heart of social and economic policy. It refers to the universal entitlement for all young people in Wales. While staff in Careers Wales may specialise in working with adults or young people, they can work with either or both, and may be found in Learndirect centres and one-stop shops.

There is less information or opinion about Careers Scotland, largely because this organisation felt itself unable to receive a visit from the OECD team at that point so early in its development. There are references, however, to the developing situation in Northern Ireland and the place of careers officers working in schools and elsewhere.

As might be expected, the report stresses the wide variety of career guidance in the public employment service (where many staff might be providing career guidance without necessarily recognising that they are doing so), IAG partnerships, trade unions, Learndirect and Careers Services in higher education. A major policy issue identified for the UK government is to improve the qualifications and training needed for lifelong guidance.

One of the distinctive features of career guidance noted by OECD is the well-developed institutional support framework which is often taken for granted in the United Kingdom. This includes the National Information Advice and Guidance Board, set up by the Department of Education and Skills and the Department for Work and Pensions to ensure co-ordination of policy and provision for adults and young people and the Guidance Council, a registered charity representing a range of organisations interested in career guidance.

The Institute of Career Guidance represents career guidance practitioners and has a role in policy, advocacy and lobbying on behalf of its members. It operates a professional register and a programme of professional development. The Institute is also a founder member of the Federation of Professional Associations for Guidance, an umbrella body representing practitioners' groups over a wide spectrum, including the National Association for Educational Guidance for Adults and the National Association of Careers and Guidance Teachers. The Association of Graduate Careers Advisory Services represents higher education services and operates a code of practice, including quality assurance.

The Employment National Training Organisation sets training standards for guidance, counselling, psychotherapy and mediation. It is responsible for national vocational qualifications (NVQs) in career guidance. The Institute of Career Guidance is the awarding body for the qualification in careers guidance (the successor to the diploma in careers guidance), which is available at a range of universities throughout the United Kingdom.

Recent additions to the structural framework include the National Association of Connexions Partnerships, which appointed a chief executive in April 2003, and Careers England, a trade association of remaining Careers Companies, which also has an interest in policy and advocacy.

The knowledge base for career guidance in the UK is provided by the field itself and a number of other organisations, among them the National Institute for Careers Education and Counselling, and the Centre for Guidance Studies at the University of Derby. The university departments providing courses leading to the Qualification for Careers Guidance and a range of postgraduate diplomas, certificates and masters-level degrees also contribute to this support network. The decision to establish a National Research Forum completes the picture.

In general the OECD believes that, compared to most OECD countries, career guidance is very highly developed in the United Kingdom. More needs to be done to improve transparency: this is related to the titles and qualifications of those who work in career guidance. There is a need to ensure that career guidance retains a strong and independent identity.

It sometimes seems, however, that as the government continues with its policy of 'joined-up' services, career guidance for young people in England becomes more obscure as its strong and independent identity recedes under Connexions.

The latest initiative in social policy for young people is the Green Paper presented to Parliament in September 2003. *Every Child Matters* (HM Treasury 2003) is aimed at improving child protection. In his foreword, the Prime Minister refers to the case of Victoria Climbié and Lord Laming's enquiry into her tragic death. The paper therefore concentrates on four main themes: supporting families and carers, intervention and protection, accountability and integration, and the people working with children.

While the existing services concerned with child protection are central to the Green Paper, there is also a focus on the universal services which children use and, as the age group includes those aged up to 19, this includes Connexions. The use of the word 'universal' in this context is interesting in the light of the debate within the service about how far it is justified in concentrating its efforts on a relatively small part of the population of young people choosing careers and preparing for work.

Under the heading 'Where we want to get to', the Green Paper reports that consultation with children revealed that the five outcomes of policy which matter most are: being healthy, staying safe, enjoying and achieving, making a positive contribution and economic well-being. Economic well-being is particularly relevant to Connexions, especially as it is later translated to 'overcoming socio-economic disadvantages to achieve their full potential in life'. It is difficult to trace this theme throughout the report. There are references to relieving child poverty but none to career choice or preparation for work. Connexions is mentioned fairly frequently, for example it appears in the information hub as part of local and regional arrangements and as providing the personal advisers who are 'lead professionals' for many in the 13–19 age group. But there is only a passing reference to Connexions in the consultation questions and that concerns an administrative matter: the alignment of geographical structures with those of Children's Trusts.

The Green Paper might well involve Connexions in a number of administrative questions, continuing the historical problem of uncertain administrative arrangements which has beset career guidance services from the outset. Bringing together one example of 'joined-up' government, Connexions, with another, Children's Trusts, may result in administrative complexities too extreme to leave alone.

The decision to legislate to create a post of Director of Children's Services within local authorities is arguably the most radical in *Every Child Matters*. The section on accountability includes the government's aim that 'in the long term [they will] aim to integrate lay services for children and young people as part of Children's Trusts. These bring together local authority education and children's social services, some children's health services, Connexions and can include other services'.

Some local authorities have already moved in this direction. Essex is one, where the influential Liz Railton is responsible for learning and social care. It will be interesting to see whether she and other chief officers might make a case for positioning Connexions directly under the Director of Children's Services, as the Careers Service was placed in the department of the Director of Education from 1994. Elected members of local authorities will also have a view. Sir Sandy Bruce Lockhart, also regarded as influential, will become chairman of the Local Government Association in 2004. This Association was instrumental in keeping the Youth Service out of Connexions, ensuring that it remained a local authority service.

More pressing than the administrative positioning of Connexions will be the function it performs. It would be possible, for example, to see the service take some over-arching responsibility for the 13–19 age group, while health and education services performed the same function for pre-school and children between 5 and 13. More satisfactory for those who believe that Connexions should develop its Careers Service role would be to make it a truly universal service taking responsibility for economic well-being and helping young people achieve their full potential.

Whilst it is important to consider the administrative and functional implications for Connexions of *Every Child Matters*, any actual changes in these areas will take place some time in the future, after the consultation process has taken place. Much more urgent is the need to consider the still-developing role of the Connexions personal adviser.

The Green Paper's chapter on workforce reform makes clear the government's intention to proceed on the lines already familiar to those in schools, social care, the police and especially the National Health Service. It looks towards common occupational standards and a common core of training. The intention is to set up a Children's Workforce Unit based in the Department for Education and Skills and later establish a Sector Skills Council for Children and Young People's Services.

The greatest care will be required over the whole sector. It could be argued that the generic principle introduced into social work thirty years ago, and the consequent withdrawal of specialist children's officers, contributed to the confusion and lack of accountability so apparent from Lord Laming's report on the tragic case of Victoria Climbié.

The workforce is huge. It includes 630,000 school staff, 40,000 in social work and 71,500 health workers. Of more direct interest to Connexions are the 3,000 education welfare officers, the 7,000 youth workers and their relationship with Connexions' own 7,000 personal advisers. Overlapping roles and common elements between education welfare officers, learning mentors and personal advisers are identified.

The Department for Education and Skills (DfES) is already aware of the need for clarity of role and title. Nowhere is this more apparent than in the case of the personal adviser. Young people, parents, teachers and others working with young people need to be able to identify the worker who can advise expertly on careers, who knows about jobs and is in contact with employers, trainers and colleges. Those who manage Connexions from the Connexions Service National Unit within the DfES have been very wary about the use of the word 'careers', perhaps because they fear it might be interpreted as denoting 'posh jobs'. They also seem devoted to the original concept of the general practitioner identified by Geoff Mulgan (now the government's head of policy) and the Social Exclusion Unit. As Connexions gains experience and knowledge, it should be capable of making its own decisions on the job titles of its workforce. But in the light of *Every Child Matters* and the warnings from the OECD more needs to be done to improve transparency and the titles of those who work in career guidance.

The Institute of Career Guidance, the Guidance Council and others will be ready to make their response. Two relative newcomers will also have valuable contributions to make. One is Careers England, the trade association of the remaining Careers Companies who provide services for Connexions partnerships. The other is the National Association of Connexions Partnerships.

The National Association was formed in January 2003 and is the natural successor to the Careers Service National Association. It represents the views of Connexions partnerships and will provide a focus for consultation. The Board of Directors, drawn from all the English regions, and the executive director should provide a corporate and much needed voice for the still new Connexions service.

Careers England, also formed early in 2003, represents sixteen Careers Companies. It is a trade association which offers a powerful voice in future policy development to organisations providing career guidance to young people and adults. Its first policy paper begins with the government's manifesto commitment to develop Careers Services and stresses the public and private good which career guidance can provide. Supported by Professors Bob Fryer, Tony Watts and Mike Campbell, and with directors drawn from prominent careers companies, it is well-placed to offer valuable advice to the government over the range of economic, educational and social policies to which Careers Services can contribute.

It is, of course, far too early to speculate on the outcomes from *Every Child Matters*, or even to suggest how the consultation process might affect the way the Connexions service is enabled to carry out its statutory duty to provide career guidance to young people under the age of 19 in England.

What seems certain is that the DfES, Ivan Lewis, the Under Secretary of State for Skills and Vocational Education, and those who advise him in the Connexions Service National Unit will be developing their own strategies in the light of *Every Child Matters*, the 14–19 Green Paper, the OECD Country Report and the various signs that interest in careers education and guidance is again growing.

Some insight into their thinking can be found in Ivan Lewis' address to the Institute of Career Guidance annual conference. No transcript of the speech is available but a report prepared for a future edition of *Career Guidance Today* (Hopkins 2003) provides a useful summary.

Lewis began in encouraging vein by emphasising the government's commitment to ensuring the availability of high quality information, advice and guidance to young people and adults. In reviewing Connexions development, he emphasised the need to ensure that young people are enabled to overcome barriers to learning but said that Connexions is much more than a youth support service for the disaffected. He stressed his determination that all young people should receive the support they need to achieve their potential. He described the proposals set out in the response to the 14–19 White Paper: 'Connexions brings to the table its expertise in offering impartial information, advice and guidance which goes beyond the professional expertise of teachers' (Hopkins 2003).

This is very reassuring to those who believe that the first objective of careers work should be to restore the highly productive partnership between teachers and career advisers threatened by the introduction of 'focusing' in 1997. It should also go some way to assure partners such as the Association of Colleges that young people should have access to impartial advice from personal advisers (careers) who are not teachers.

But it is always necessary to pay close attention to the language Mr Lewis uses to describe careers education and guidance. The same problems arise from this speech as became evident from his answers to questions raised in the House of Commons debate on the 14–19 Green Paper (quoted earlier in this Addendum). There he said that the service should be universal but he appeared to confuse careers education and careers guidance. In his address to the Institute of Career Guidance, he seemed to confuse careers education, careers information and career guidance. He referred to schools as key partners in the delivery of the universal service. Schools have a critical role to play but the question of universality is usually asked of Connexions. Referring to concern about limited access for the majority because of the focus on those not in employment, education and training, he denied this was the case.

Mr Lewis seemed to cloud this issue further by quoting Connexions Direct and 'high quality information, advice and guidance through telephone, Internet and interactive media' (Hopkins 2003). Connexions Direct can contribute when giving careers information and general advice. But it is not pedantic to question how far career guidance needs can adequately be met by telephone The concern noted by Mr Lewis is usually expressed by teachers, young people and parents unable to get personal access to a personal adviser skilled in giving impartial career guidance one-to-one.

In conclusion the Under Secretary of State called for a fundamental culture change within Connexions: improved client access, an integrated service for adults through information advice and guidance services and Learndirect; and for readily available labour market information. He pointed out that Connexions and information advice and guidance services have led the way in showing how public service can be modernised and reformed.

These conclusions are intriguing. Culture change in the excellent organisation is brought about by dialogue between managers and staff: in this case, the dedicated body of practitioners who have been able to exert influence so successfully in the past. A debate on the OECD report might be the best place to start. If Careers Services lead the way in public service reform, the challenge to government is to ensure that they are able to do so while retaining the strong and independent identity emphasised by the OECD.

The history of Careers Services in the United Kingdom has not altered direction in the first year of its second century. It would be surprising if it had. What is already apparent is that interest remains strong and continues to increase, especially at a global level. The balance between social, educational and economic influences continues to shift as it has since the beginning of its first century.

The administrative framework is now characterised by diversity. Careers Services differ throughout the United Kingdom and it is from difference we learn.

Bibliography

Association of Education Committees (1983) 'MSC The First Decade,' *Education Digest*, July.

Association of Juvenile Employment and Welfare Officers (1928) *Onward*, vol. 1, part 9, Editorial. Magazine of the Association of Juvenile Employment and Welfare Officers.

Avent, C. (1976) *Careering Along: Careers Guidance*, London: Batsford Books.

—— (1997) 'Looking Back: Where We Were Then!,' *Newscheck*, Department for Education and Employment, vol. 8, no. 3, p.9.

Bayliss, V. (1994) Interview, *Career Guidance Today*, summer, p.10.

—— (1995) 'Opening the Door to Let the Future In,' *Careers Guidance Today*, winter.

—— (1997) *Key Views on the Future of Work*, London: Royal Society of Arts.

—— (1999) *Joined up Guidance: Where do we go from here?*, Derby: Centre for Guidance Studies.

Bentley, T. and Gurumurthy, R. (1999) *Destination Unknown: Engaging with the Problems of Marginalised Youth*, London: Demos.

—— and Oakley, J. (1999) *The Real Deal*, London: Demos.

Bereznicki, C. (1997) 'The View from Here,' *Careers Guidance Today*, summer, vol. 5, no. 2.

Bezanson, L. (2001) 'Policy in Practice,' *Career Guidance Today*, Sept/Oct 2001, vol. 9, no. 5.

Blackstone, T. House of Lords, Hansard vol. 610, no. 51.

Blair, A. (1995) 'The *Spectator* Lecture,' *Guardian*, 22 Feb.

Blunkett, D. (2000) *Education into Employability*, London: Department for Education and Employment.

Booker, C. (1979) *The Seventies*, London: Penguin.

Bradley, S. (1990) 'The Careers Service Past, Present and Future,' *British Journal of Guidance and Counselling*, vol. 18, no. 2, May.

Byers, S. (1996) *The Opposition View*, Institute of Careers Guidance conference report, Stourbridge: Institute of Careers Guidance.

—— and Gee, R. (1995) *A Successful Career: Careers Services in the Twenty-first Century*, unpublished draft Labour Party policy statement.

Careers and Occupational Information Centre (COIC) (1980) *Preparing for Employment or Unemployment*, London: COIC.

Cherry, N. (1974) 'Components of Occupational Interest,' *British Journal of Education and Counselling*, vol. 2, no. 1.

—— (1974a) *Research for the Medical Research Council*, London: London School of Economics.

Chubb, P. (1994) 'Achieving a National Council,' a personal (unpublished) paper, May.

—— (1996) 'Report of the Presidential Select Committee,' (unpublished) Stourbridge: Institute of Careers Guidance.

Collins, T. (1986) 'Careers Officer 2000,' *Careers Journal*, vol. 6, no 3.

—— (1989) 'Do it Different,' *The Careers Officer*, winter.

—— (2001) 'A Professional Guarantee: How a Register of Practitioners Helps Clients,' *Career Guidance Today*, Nov/Dec, vol. 9, no. 6.

—— and Peck, D. (1973) 'The Chartered Careers Officer,' *Youth Employment*, winter.

CRAC/NICEC (Careers Research and Advisory Centre/National Institute of Careers Education) (2001) 'Lifelong Guidance for Economic and Social Success,' conference briefing for Home International 2, June.

CSNA (Careers Service National Association) (1999) *'Learning to Succeed' and the SEU's 'Bridging the Gap,'* Winchester: CSNA.

—— (2000) *Position Paper on Learning and Skills Bill*, Winchester: CSNA.

CSNU (Connexions Service National Unit) (2002) *Connexions Business Planning Guidance 2003–2004*, Sheffield: CSNU.

David, T. (1966) 'Albemarle and After,' *Youth Employment*, summer.

Davies, B. (1999) *A History of the Youth Service 1939–1999*, Leicester: Youth Work Press.

Davis, H. (1995) 'For Better for Worse,' *Careers Guidance Today*, winter, p. 7.

Daws, P.P. (1966) *A Good Start in Life*, Cambridge: CRAC.

Department for Education and Employment (DfEE) *Better Choices*, London: DfEE.

—— (1995/96) *Annual Report on the Careers Service*, London: DfEE.

—— (1996) 'Shaping the Future: Conference Report,' internal report, London: DfEE.

—— (1996a) 'The Role of Choice and Careers Division,' *Newscheck*, Nov., vol. 7.

—— (1997) *Learning and Working Together for the Future*, London: DfEE.

—— (1997a) 'Guidance Through Partnership,' *Newscheck*, vol. 8, no. 3.

—— (1997b) *The Report of the Chief Inspector on the Work of the Careers Service 1996/1997*, London: DfEE.

—— (DfEE) (1997c) *Contracting out of Careers Services in England*, National Audit Office report, London: DfEE.

—— (1997d) *The Careers Service: Annual Report 1996–97*, London: DfEE.

—— (1997e) *The Requirements and Guidance for Careers Services*, Sheffield: DfEE.

—— (1998) *Local Information, Advice and Guidance for Adults in England: Towards a National Framework*, London: DfEE.

—— (1998a) 'Taking Forward Careers Service Focusing in Schools,' Choice and Careers Division, internal report, London: DfEE.

—— (1999) *Bridging the Gap: New Opportunities for 16 Year Olds Not in Education*, report of the Social Exclusion Unit, London: DfEE.

—— (1999a) *Learning to Succeed: A New Framework for Learning*, London: DfEE.

—— (2000) *The Connexions Service: Prospectus and Specification*, London: DfEE.

—— (2000a) *The Connexions Service: Professional Framework for Personal Advisers and Proposal for Consultation*, London: DfEE.

—— (2000b) 'The Connexions Service and Schools,' internal circular, London: DfEE.

—— (2000c) *Connexions: The Best Start in Life for Every Young Person*, London: DfEE.

—— (2001) *A Review of Careers Service Focusing in Schools*, QPID study report no. 93, Sheffield: DfEE.

Department for Education and Skills (DfES) (2003) *Careers Education and Guidance in England: A National Framework 11–19*, London: DfES.

Department of Employment (DE) (1965) *The Future of the Youth Employment Service* (Albemarle Report), London: HMSO.

—— (1971) *People and Jobs: A Modern Employment Service*, London: DE.

—— (1973) *The Employment and Training Act 1973: The Careers Service*, London: DE.

—— (1974) *The Careers Service: Guidance to LEAs in England and Wales*, London: HMSO.

—— (1979) 'The Developing Role of the DE Careers Service Branch,' *Careers Bulletin*, p.10.

—— (1980) *The Careers Service: Guidance to LEAs in England and Wales* (1980 revision), London: HMSO.

—— (1984) *Careers Service Branch Annual Report on the Careers Service*, London: DE.

—— (1984a) *Better Choices*, London: DE with Department for Education.

—— (1993) Letter to Chief Education Officers dated 28 July 1993 from the head of Careers Service Branch.

—— (1993a) *Requirements and Guidance for Providers* (Introduction), provided to contractors, London: DE.

Devine, K. (1981) Presidential Address to Institute of Careers Guidance Annual Conference, unpublished copy held in ICG archive.

Dick, D. (1994) 'Dick's Diary,' *Careers Guidance Today*, autumn, p.10.

Dowson, H. and Peck, D. (1964) 'Careers Guidance in a Mixed Secondary School,' *Youth Employment*, spring.

Dryden, W. and Watts, A. (1991) *Guidance and Counselling in Britain: A 20-Year Perspective*, Cambridge: Hobsons.

Duncan, W. (1951) 'The Vocational Guidance of Disabled Young People,' *Occupational Psychology*.

Durham County Council (1937) *Handbook for the Use of Officers in Juvenile Employment Bureaux*, Durham: Durham County Council.

Eastwood, M. and Peck, D. (1995) 'Towards 2000,' *Careers Guidance Today*, winter, vol. 3, no. 4.

Ford, G. (2002) *The Connexions Strategy and All-age Guidance*, Derby: Centre for Guidance Studies.

Foster, H. (1965) 'The Derby Labourers Hire 1903,' *Youth Employment*, vol XVII, no. 2.

Greenwell, E.G. (1964) *A History of the National Association of Youth Employment Officers*, Stourbridge: Institute of Youth Employment Officers.

Guidance Council (1999) *The Guidance Council's Response to the 'Learning to Succeed' White Paper*, London: Guidance Council.

—— (2000) Policy Bulletin, no. 7, London: Guidance Council.

—— (2000a) Policy Bulletins nos 1–13, London: Guidance Council.

Hayden, H. and Heathcote, J. (1964) 'The Carter Lodge Experiment,' *Youth Employment*, spring.

Heginbotham, H. (1951) *The Youth Employment Service*, Norwich: Jarrald & Sons Ltd.

Her Majesty's Treasury (2003) *Every Child Matters*, London: HM Treasury.

Hicks, M. (2001) *Careers Work and Independent Schools 1920–2000*, prepared for the Independent Schools Careers Organisation.

Hoggart, R. (1959) *The Uses of Literacy*, London: Pelican Books.

—— (1995) *The Way We Live Now*, London: Pimlico.

Hopkins, L. (2002) *Career Guidance in Northern Ireland: A Service in Transition*, Institute of Career Guidance briefing paper, July, unpublished.

—— (2003) 'Provision through Partnership: a Report on a Speech by Ivan Lewis, MP, Under Secretary of State for Skills and Vocational Education, given to the Institute of Career Guidance,' *Write Now*, September.

Howden, R. and Peck, D. (1980) *Careers Guidance in the 1980s*, occasional paper, Sheffield: COIC.

Howells, K. (1997) 'Guidance Through Partnership Speech,' unpublished transcript of his speech, London: DfEE.

Hulme, D. (1972) Editorial, *Careers Quarterly*, autumn.

Hurst, R. (1977) 'The Careers Service of the Future,' *Careers Quarterly*, autumn.

—— (1985) 'Retiring Address of the Honorary Secretary,' *Careers Quarterly*, autumn, vol. 29, no. 2.

Hutton, W. (1995) *The State We're In*, London: Vintage Original.

Innes, P.D. (1932) *The Role of Vocational Tests as Aids to Choice of Employment*, City of Birmingham Education Committee.

Institute of Careers Guidance (ICG) (1971) Correspondence between C. P. Walton and Neil Kinnock M.P. regarding local authority associations and the Institute of Careers Officers, held in ICG archive.

—— (1990) Report of an ICG Council Meeting with Geoffrey Holland, *The Careers Officer*, Institute of Careers Officers, summer.

—— (1996) *Careers Guidance for Adults*, Stourbridge: Institute of Careers Guidance.

—— (1997) Response from the Institute of Careers Guidance to 'Learning and Working Together for the Future,' Stourbridge: Institute of Career Guidance.

—— (1998) Conference Report, *Careers Guidance Today*, autumn, vol. 6, no. 3, p. 21.

—— (1999) *Learning to Succeed* (The Institute response to the White Paper and the SEU report *Bridging the Gap*), Stourbridge: Institute of Career Guidance.

—— (2000) 'Implementing Inclusiveness: Proposals of the Beattie Committee,' *Careers Guidance Today*, vol. 8, no. 3.

—— (2002) *Career Guidance: One Aim, Three Routes*, Institute of Career Guidance briefing paper, Stourbridge: ICG.

—— and National Association of Careers and Guidance Teachers (1994) *Certain to Succeed*, a joint policy paper, Stourbridge: ICG.

—— (1992) UK Heads of Career Service Association, Training Enterprise Councils Chief Executives Network, *Delivering Quality Careers Guidance*, Stourbridge: ICG.

Institute of Careers Officers (ICO) (1987), *Proposed Code of Practice*, London: ICO.

—— (1987a) *Proposed Code of Practice for Careers Guidance*, London: ICO.

—— (1988) 'Lamorbey Park 48: 40 Years On,' *Careers Quarterly*, winter, vol. 9, no. 11.

—— (1990) The Conference Report, *The Careers Officer*, p.19.

Institute of Manpower Studies (IMS) (1984) *Competence and Competition*, London: Institute of Manpower Studies.

Jackson, C., Watts, A. and Hughes, D. (2001) *Careers Service Work with Adults: A Survey*, Centre for Guidance Studies, occasional paper.

Jenkins, R. (2001) *Churchill*, London: Pan Books.

Johnson, A. (1981) 'How Can We Manage?,' *In Service Training*, Local Government Management Board, June.

Jones, S. (1999) Report, *Times Educational Supplement*, 1 Oct. 1999.

Killeen, J. and Kidd, J. (1996) *The Careers Service: Re-thinking Careers Education and Guidance*, London: Routledge.

Law, B. (2001) *New Thinking for Connexions and Citizenship*, London: Centre for Guidance Studies occasional paper.

Lawrence, D. (1993) *The Rise and Fall of the Local Government Careers Service*, University of Birmingham: Institute of Local Government Studies, 1993.

Lewis, I. (2002) 'Driving Connexions Forward,' *Career Guidance Today*, Jan./Feb., vol. 10, no. 1.

Little, R. and Peck, D. (1986) 'Gap in the Jigsaw,' *Times Educational Supplement*, 25 July.

—— 'In Danger of Overkill,' *Times Educational Supplement*, 7 Oct.

—— (1995) 'Clearing a Path for a Wider Age Group,' *Times Educational Supplement*, 2 Aug.

McGowan, A. (1995) 'A Vision of the Future,' *Careers Guidance Today*, winter, vol. 3, no. 4.

McLeod, J. (1989) 'Bring on the Trojan Horses,' *Education*, Association of Education Committees.

Manpower Services Commission (MSC) (1977) *Young People and Work*, Sheffield: MSC.

—— (1981) *A New Training Initiative*, Sheffield: MSC.

Milsted, G. (1960) *Memoranda and Reminiscence 1910–1960*, self published.

Ministry of Labour (1945) *Report of the Committee on the Juvenile Employment Service*, London: HMSO.

NAJEWO (1928) 'Nestor' Editorial, *NAJEWO Magazine*, vol. 1, part 9.

National Association of Youth Employment Officers (NAYEO) (1949), *Youth Employment Officers Bulletin* (May), Stourbridge: NAYEO (ICG archive).

National Institute for Careers Education and Counselling (NICEC) (1992), *Economic Benefits of Careers Guidance*, NICEC briefing, Cambridge: NICEC.

Nicholson, P. (2002) (Chairman of Zacchaeus Trust), 'New Views on an Age Old Question,' *Guardian*, 13 May, p. 19.

Organisation for Economic Co-operation and Development (OECD), *Review of Career Guidance Policies: United Kingdom Country Note*, London: OECD.

OFSTED (2002) *Connexions Partnerships: The First Year 2001–2002*, London: Office for Standards in Education.

Paice, J. (1995) 'An Address to ICG Senior Managers Conference 1995,' *Careers Guidance Today*, summer, p. 20.

Pawinska, B. (2000) 'Note from the Chief Executive,' *Careers Guidance Today*, winter.

Pearce, N., and Hillman, J. (1999) *Wasted Youth: Raising Achievement and Tackling Social Exclusion*, London: Institute for Public Policy Research.

Peck, D. (1975) 'The Careers Officer and the Careers Teacher,' *Careers Quarterly*, 1975, vol. 26, no. 4.

—— (1975a) 'The New Careers Service Eighteen Months On,' *Careers Adviser*.

—— (1979) 'Working Together: local authorities and DfEE,' *Local Government Journal*, Association of Municipal Authorities.

—— (1979a) 'Keeping School Leavers out of the Dole Queue,' *Municipal Review*, Association of Municipal Authorities.

—— (1979b) *County Councils Gazette: Careers 1979*, London: Association of County Councils.

—— (1981) 'A Newer Initiative,' *Times Educational Supplement*, 11 Sept.

—— and Hurst, R. (1983) *Guide to Careers Work*, National Union of Teachers, London: NUT.

—— (1984) 'Operation Overlord,' *Times Educational Supplement*, 24 Feb.

—— (1984a) *Education and Vocational Counselling for Adults*, NICEC training bulletin, Cambridge: NICEC.

—— (1985) 'The Significance of Competence and Competition,' *Education*, Feb.

—— (1986) 'The Careers Service after Inlogov,' *Education*, Association of Education Committees, 9 May.

—— (1988) 'How Can we Manage Better?,' *In Service Training*, Sept.

—— (1992) 'Guidance and the New Right,' *The Careers Officer*, Institute of Careers Officers, spring.

—— (1992a) 'Guidance and the New Right,' *National Association of Careers and Guidance Teachers Journal*, Apr.

—— (1995) 'The Shape of Things to Come,' *Careers Guidance Today*, autumn.

—— (1995a) 'Leading the Way,' *Careers Guidance Today*, vol. 4, no. 2.

Jackson, M. (1992) 'Preserving Norman's Architecture,' *Times Educational Supplement* (Editorial), 12 Jan., p. 15.

Prentice, B. (1996) 'Careers under Labour,' Careers Guidance Today, vol. 4, no. 4.

Ranson, S. and Ribbins, P. (1985) *Servicing Careers in the Post-employment Society*, Institute of Local Government Studies, University of Birmingham, 1985. London: Falmer.

Rimmer, A. (1989) Editorial, *Careers Quarterly*, vol. 30, no. 3.

Roberts, K. (1971) *From School to Work: A Study of the Youth Employment Service*, Newton Abbott: David and Charles.

—— (1984) *School Leavers and their Prospects*, Milton Keynes: Open University Press.

—— (1995) 'Recurrent Guidance for Prolonged Transitions,' *Careers Guidance Today*, winter.

—— (2000) 'Cause for Optimism,' *Careers Guidance Today*, Sept./Oct., vol. 8, no. 5.

—— (2001) *Class in Modern Britain*, London: Palgrave.

Robertson, R. (1996) *The Government View*, Scottish Officer Education Minister, ICG Conference Report, unpublished, distributed to ICG members only.

Robinson F., and Peck, D., *The Revolution in Education and Training*, London: Longman.

Rodger, A. (1961) unpublished lecture, Lamorbey Park, held in ICG archive.

—— (1968) [1950] *The Seven-point Plan*, London: National Institute of Individual Psychology.

Sadler, J. (1997) 'Looking Back: Careers Information Then and Now,' *Newscheck*, Department for Education and Employment, vol. 8, no. 3, p.8.

Sheffield Education Committee (1951) *Annual Report on the Youth Employment Service*, Sheffield: Sheffield Education Committee.

—— (1955–6) *Annual Report on the Youth Employment Service 1955–56*, Sheffield: Sheffield Education Committee.

Showler, B. (1976) *The Public Employment Service*, London: Longman.

Simpson, P. (1997) *The Internal Labour Market*, London: Royal Society of Arts.

Smith, P. (1911) 'Thoughts for a Boy on Choosing Work,' Edinburgh: Edinburgh School Board.

Smith, P. (1940) Bulletin (January), National Association of Juvenile Employment and Welfare Officers, ICG archive.

Smith, P. (1951) 'Twenty-five Years of Research in Vocational Guidance,' *Occupational Psychology*, Jan., vol. XXV, no.1, held in ICG archive.

Society of Education Officers (1980) *The Careers Service: Guidance to LEAs*, London: Society of Education Officers.

Super, D. (1985) 'Self-realisation through Work and Leisure Roles,' *Educational and Vocational Guidance Bulletin, 43/85*, International Association of Educational and Vocational Guidance.

Surridge, O. (1987) 'Careering Towards Equal Opportunities,' *Education*, 25 Sept.

Taylor, C. (1988) 'Professionalism: Time to Take Stock,' *Careers Journal*, vol. 8, no. 3.

UK Heads of Careers Service Group (1992) Memorandum to all Heads of Careers Services, Winchester: UK Heads of Careers Service Group.

Walton, C.P. (1971) 'People and Jobs,' unpublished paper for members of the ICO.

—— (1973) 'Where to when LEAs take over?,' *Times Educational Supplement*, 16 March.

—— (1981) 'Then and Now,' *Careers Quarterly*, autumn.

Watts, A.G. (1984) *Work Experience in Schools*, London: Heinemann.

—— (1984a) *Education, Unemployment and the Future of Work*, London: Heinemann.

—— (1991) 'The Impact of the New Right Policy Challenges Confronting Guidance in England and Wales,' *British Journal of Guidance and Counselling*, Sept., vol. 19, no. 3.

—— (1994) 'Lifelong Guidance for Lifelong Career Development,' *Careers Guidance Today*, winter, p. 21.

—— (1996) 'Socio-political Ideologies in Guidance,' in A.G. Watts, R. Hawthorn, J. Kidd, J. Killeen and B. Law (eds) *Rethinking Careers Education and Guidance*, London: Routledge.

—— (1996a) 'Careers Work in Higher Education,' *Rethinking Careers Education and Guidance*, London: Routledge.

—— (1997) 'Careerquake,' *Careers Guidance Today*, autumn (Taken from an earlier book with the same name from Demos).

—— (1999) 'Career Guidance and Public Policy,' *Career Guidance Today*, Sept./Oct., vol. 7, no. 4.

—— (2000) 'Connexions Origins and Prospects,' speech to National Association of Careers and Guidance Teachers, Annual Conference, July.

—— (2001) 'Career Guidance and Social Exclusion: A Cautionary Tale,' *British Journal of Guidance and Counselling*, vol. 29, no. 2.

—— (2002) 'International Comparisons: Drawing the Strings Together,' *Career Guidance Today*, Oct., vol. 10, no. 5.

Weinstock, A. (2001) *Connexions and Youth Policy: A Brighter Future*, Centre for Guidance Studies, University Of Derby, Nov. 2001.

Welsh National Assembly (2000) *'Supporting Young People in Wales,' Statement by the First Secretary*, Dec., Cardiff: Welsh National Assembly.

White, P. (1981) 'One Approach to Management,' *In Service Training*, Sept.

Wicks, M. (2000) 'Wicks' Way To Lifelong Learning,' *Careers Guidance Today*, vol. 7, no. 5, p. 15.

—— (2000a) House of Commons, Hansard col. 520, March.

Widdecombe, A. (1994) 'Vision into Practice,' *Careers Guidance Today*, winter, p. 14.

Williams, S. (1966) 'Future Development of the YES,' *Youth Employment*, Institute of Youth Employment Officers.

Wintour, P. (2002) 'Birt Seeks New Way for Transport,' *Guardian*, 8 Jan., p. 4.

Wylie, T. (2000) 'Widening the Vision,' *Careers Guidance Today*, Sept./Oct. 2000, vol. 8 no. 5.

Index